SELFLESS

TURIYA: BEYOND THE DARK NIGHT OF THE SOUL

JAI

SELFLESS

TURIYA: BEYOND THE DARK NIGHT OF THE SOUL

SELFLESS: Turiya – Beyond the Dark Night of the Soul

by JAI (Dream Universal Media)

Copyright © 2016-2018 by JAI

ISBN-13: 978-1-7324068-5-8

Edited by: Timothy Rodd and The Night Shift Editing Team

Disclaimer

The materials contained in this text are provided for the purpose of general information only and do not constitute professional medical or psychological advice. The author/publisher accepts no responsibility for any loss which may arise from ill-advised reliance on, and/or practice of information contained herein. The author will arrange Q&A sessions if any are needed after reading this manual.

Meditation is generally considered a safe activity, especially at the beginning levels. At these levels, it is mainly an exercise in relaxation and concentration. However, the advanced levels of meditation can require a willingness to use your powers of concentration in order to engage in self-study and examination. If you feel you might be uncomfortable engaging in this kind of self-examination, then I ask that you do not proceed beyond the beginning level until you feel secure and comfortable with going further.

If you have a history of mental illness, then please consult with your health care provider before learning meditation. This is not to say that meditation will be harmful to you, but it's better to be on the safe side.

Please be aware that I make no claim to be a psychologist, therapist, counselor, or medical professional. Anything I say or write should be understood as my own opinion and not an expression of professional advice or prescription. You are entirely responsible for how you choose to understand, misunderstand, use or misuse any of my writings or communications.

I can accept no responsibility for any adverse effects, direct or indirect, that may result from your use of the information on this website or in any of my communications. Furthermore, I make no guarantees that any of the information or practices on this website or that I may write about will function in any particular way for you. By using this website, you agree that you use the information contained here-in entirely at your own discretion.

Consecration

May the words of my mouth and the meditations of my heart be acceptable to the Most High, Creator of all the worlds and Timeless realms. I pray that my will and Thy Will are as One. I write from that Oneness.

I offer this book in the Name of the One Holy True and Living God, from Whom all emanate and` to Whom all returns. It is important to our soul's illumination that we know our Oneness with The Divine, and live from that place in consciousness. It is a breach of reason to perpetuate the divisive labels we may seek to assign and define That Which Created all things. We are One.

My soul is thankful for The Protection, Love, and Guidance of The Comforter, The God, The Holy Spirit. I accept that the Faces that have been shown to us as Manifestations of The Creator, known and unknown, seen and unseen, were and are among us.

I offer this journal from no position of authority. I am but a traveler. I am a student, a seeker, lifting my pen and voice to express praise and thanks to The Almighty, the Most High, for the blessing of this opportunity to share this journey with you.

I accept that the Holy Names of The God and the Holy Attributes of The God, both known and unknown, know nothing of contradiction in opposites of polarities, only the Union of Spirit. All gender references to The God in this text reflect terminology that is not necessarily intended to be gender-specific. Both the Yin and the Yang energies must exist to be our cause and continuation. The masculine and feminine energies are compelled to engage in this grand mystical dance of existence equally respected and acknowledged as being mutually responsible for the emanation of all creation in its myriad glorious forms. The God is called by many names from many traditions. My focus remains on The One … That which defies our marginalized, limited comprehension, that which cannot be named, known, or defined.

Acknowledgments

I thank The Most High for visions of the other side for evidence that there is no "veil" between worlds. You showed me that the realm of Maya was just the tip of the iceberg. You smiled Transcendence upon me from one dimension into the next. Thank you for stepping through the portal to the Mystic Realm and showing me that this is not all there is.

I thank my mother, Dorothy Raushanna Hassain, the sunshine of my life, for teaching me that there is no such thing as a one-dimensional world. Your life still breathes through me. You are one of the most powerful Natural Mystics I have ever known. I am so grateful to you for all of the love you brought to my life. I thank The God every day for ever having been blessed to know you and love you.

Matthias Swaby – I thank you for your prayers. Your life is a testament to the power of The God over life and death. I thank The God for you and for the spiritual intervention that performed a profound healing in my life. I can never repay you for your bravery, persistence, and courage, fearlessly confronting demons with the touch of an angel of The God. Your humble manner and your chosen surrendered life are a soul's inspiration. I am blessed to have been welcomed into your spiritual family.

Timothy Rodd – Thank you for graphic designs, cover art, and management of the Night Shift Editing Team. May all of your tireless efforts to help bring this work into being be blessed and rewarded by the Powers of Light that oversee it.

Night Shift Editing Team – Thank you all for your energy, time, and diligence. As the old saying goes, "The devil is in the details." Thank you for following it through to the last breath of exorcising that beast.

The Light Meditation

Written by JAI
Tim Rodd: Narration, Copy Editing, Post Production
Levi Chen: Chinese Harp or Zither
Rahmon Muhammad: Sound Engineer
Sebastian Robertson: Sound Engineer

Turiya Meditation

Written by JAI
Tim Rodd: Copy Editing, Post Production
Levi Chen: Chinese Harp or Zither
Rahmon Muhammad: Sound Engineer
Sebastian Robertson: Sound Engineer

Many thanks to prolific composer, producer, visionary musician, and performing artist … the heart and soul of Yin Yang Records and Liquid Gardens, Levi Chen. Dream Universal extends immense appreciation, love, and light for your participation in our healing Mystical Meditation journeys. The East meets West meets the Cosmos, ethereal soundscapes of Meditation of my Soul, featuring the interplay of ambient electric guitar textures and the traditional Gu Zheng, Chinese harp, formed a sound that perfectly complements our catalog of healing meditations.

SELFLESS

TURIYA:: BEYOND THE DARK NIGHT OF THE SOUL

Table of Contents

The Dark Night of the Soul

The Dark Night of the Soul

The term Dark Night of the Soul sounds foreboding. It sounds like a soul-slaying, terrifying nightmare. It sounds ominous, sinister, and even evil. We would be missing the whole point if we believed all of that. What if I told you that it was not the end, but instead a new beginning, a cleansing, a rite of passage, a rebirth? It is not a derailment. It is a rerouting of our path on the sacred journey to our true destiny. Of course, it doesn't feel that way when it's happening. Whoever and whatever pushed us into this archetypal experience is energetically invested in our believing that this dark night is the end of every good thing about a reality that was only a dream in the first place. The day will come, when we will look back at it, fully awake, with gratitude for that intervention.

Even if we are in so much pain that we are numb, we still must affirm that our life exists as a gift of incredible potential, to be filled with love and compassion, kindness and decency, integrity and humanity, forgiveness, and mercy. I love the Persian poet and mystic, Rumi. We have been through so much together. I meditate on his words, "The cure for pain is in the pain." It is our nature to avoid pain as a survival mechanism. In the face of trauma and painful experiences, we instinctively seek every opportunity to distract, dissociate, and disconnect. In a state of "disconnect," we are rewiring our circuitry to run just as fast away from our joy. Pain is one of our greatest teachers. We can't run from it.

The primordial womb of all of creation should teach us not to be afraid of the dark. It is the dark. Our soul knows that it was from self-illuminating triple darkness that everything and everyone emerged. It is the mind that wants to analyze the concept of change to dust, as though our very existence was not based on change. The transformation from caterpillars to butterflies is a sign of the nature of immaculate and elegant metamorphosis. From the chrysalis to the spread of its beautiful wings, it is not an event. It is a process. A butterfly does not even remember being a caterpillar. It does not regret having to spin a cocoon. It does not curse the darkness from which it emerged.

What are we afraid of?
Who taught us to fear the dark ... and why?
Who taught us to associate darkness with evil ... and why?
Those two words are not synonymous
From darkness we are born, again and again
Not as the absence of, but the Creator of Light
From the womb to the tomb ... Defying the nature of creation
we are taught to fear the dark though it is the agent of our gestation
The word "dark" is too often used in disparaging terms
From it we have emerged and into it we return
Behind closed eyes, in Dream State meditation
Beyond Zero-Point Negative Existence ... Beyond the First Vibration
When I am too weary from the never-ending fight
and life has spun completely out-of-control
I will sit by Myself and love my True Self in the dark
The Dark Night of my Soul

The Dark Night of the Soul is a portal. It serves a purpose in our lives. What makes it survivable is that we know if we can just get through that night, no matter how long it takes, everything that is meant to be will be. What we seek is seeking us and will manifest as our destiny. The positive energy that we put out in the Universe will return on the wings of prayers we don't even remember praying. There is no such thing as an unanswered prayer, regardless of paradoxical appearances.

"The Dark Night of the Soul," is as much a mystical experience as it is an ill-fated, sorrowful dance with shadows, spinning out of what once was, into an abysmal realm of broken spirits and crushed dreams. A powerful force descends upon its mortally wounded victim, already ensnared in a web of sorrow, from which there seems no escape. It snuffs out the last flicker of Hope's Light as if to dare the Sun ever to rise again.

This initiatory archetypal experience suggests an existential crisis of consciousness, yet delivers the experience of Union and Oneness in the Transcendent Realms of Divinity. Even though it visits everyone, independent of religious context, it is now a cliché, secular expression. It was St. John of the Cross who coined the phrase and spiritual phenomenon of "The Dark Night of the Soul." He followed his eight-stanza poem with a twenty-three-page treatise and commentary, to communicate that his experience was not a demonstration of faithlessness. Still, it is often misinterpreted by some religious people to be a "crisis of faith" or a weakened relationship with, even a doubting, of the power of God. The "Dark Night" is not to be mistaken for a common depression or faithlessness. It is the gateway of a portal into the embrace of complete surrender. It is beyond thought, on the other side of reason, even beyond hope, to be able to navigate the torrential storms of life.

I was both blessed and troubled by many profound insights that occurred throughout the editing process of my collection of healing meditations … especially the one I named TURIYA. I was forced to revisit the energy of this section with a deeper level of empathy and compassion than I feel I had to offer it before. The section called Turiya first appeared in my book, THE TIMELESS NOW: Healing from Grief and Loss. Most of what I presented in that section involved looking outside one's Self for comfort, for survival, for hope, for healing … even for God. I suggested that somebody would *always* be there for you … somewhere. That perspective lacked the depth it deserved. The meditation, Turiya, spoke itself into existence. A transcript, instruction, and protocol booklet followed, then this book evolved from that and took on a life of its own.

I had come to realize that pure evil would have it that there would be that one night, day, moment … after that phone call, that message, that vision, that dream, that news, that guilt, that rejection, that loss, that betrayal, that memory, that pain, that aloneness … would find a place to land in the heart of my peace of mind, like a heat-seeking missile, and obliterate everything I believed to be real. It would will into being what is known as the Dark Night of the Soul. Yes, there would be that one night when there was no one. No matter what we had ever sacrificed for another, no matter what we had ever believed in, how intense our prayers, how deep our meditation, how profound our love, how confirmed our strength … that one night would be destined to come and there would be nobody … nobody there.

Imagine … Your face engulfed in the blue glow of artificial light, your radiated hand clutches a smartphone, your index finger scrolling down your list of "contacts" … a misnomer, because you are not really in *contact* with anyone on that list … not the kind of contact you need right now, for even one ray of Light, one whisper of "Don't give up." A hand, weakened by despair … clutching the "Ouiji" mouse for dear life, finger scrolling down the bottomless pit of posts and selfies on what you know for a fact now to be anti-social media, you consider your life even emptier than you previously believed.

You don't have "your best life" to demonstrate in frozen, dead-eyed, teeth skinning, cute-posing social media buddy/friend pleasing updates. Everyone is wearing the same smile, and they appear to have the same puppies. Puppies are cool. Ads, ads, ads … more things to desire to pile on top of all of the other "things" to love, none of which would ever love you back. Click "Home" and start again … You face a warm, welcome "HI whoever you are! What's on your mind? How are you feeling?" You choose the face that best matches yours for that moment. Now you are an emoji. A happy face, an angry face, a sad face, one with hearts, not X's for eyes … Oh! There! … There's a blue thumbs up that declares in a dismissive gesture that says, "I'm okay!"

I'm talking to that one precious soul, wrapped in the billowing fog of impenetrable shadows of suffocating despair, bound and gagged by the silence of that one unthinkable, unimaginable night that no one was there … or that someone you thought would be there, was not there. That one night, that the ones who are there are just too busy with their lives to lose a wink of sleep over your "issues" … silence spinning in the Ether of last breaths that didn't matter. There is not one single flicker of Light that illuminates the existential nightmare of the Dark Night of a Soul … Not one word … Not one extended hand before the third plunge underwater at the deep end of the pool happens.

Who do you call when the shock of that wave passes over you? Who or what do you call upon? What if you don't feel so "entitled" to being attended to by the angels that were set in place as our guides and protectors, because of some misplaced, conditioned guilt for being? What if you feel there's nowhere to go that will be any more welcoming than where you are? Without a shield, a mantra, an altar, a prayer … Without a friend, without a single person on the planet that knows or cares at all, one way or the other … Even without an enemy … Nothing. It is true that sometimes someone just being there is enough. But that is only determined by the reflection in the mirror of the one assumed to be present. So, it depends. Because a body is apparent, it does not mean that the essence and intention of the spirit that is in it are present. At a funeral, there is a body, but nobody is in it. What positive energy can an empty vessel offer to the waning life-force of anyone … only a new dimension of aloneness that death cannot fathom?

Trusting that we have a unique connection and relationship in Oneness with the Divine can be enough to feel secure and strong in faith, knowing that *Something* is there. *Something* powerful enough to intervene in our lives, in a personal way, is there. Beyond contradicting images, beyond a void, not just space, or nothingness.

6

What is even beyond that? Everything is there, willing and able to intervene in our affairs. True healing is even beyond that, to the extent that we are able to connect directly from unknowable realms within to transcendent realms. Our goal is to resist engaging in a fearful relationship with the Dark Night as well as the Transcendent Light of Source Energy. Instead, we seek to:

- Know what it is and observe it objectively;
- Know how it operates within each and every one of us;
- Know what triggers it;
- Know how it affects our lives;
- Know how to heal from the space we stand in;
- Embrace a spiritual practice that nurtures our soul and increases our Light;
- Transcend former limiting belief systems that embolden the ego to sabotage our lives;
- Stay as the True Self, unmoved by external circumstances.

Everyone faces soul-shattering events that can leave life in scattered pieces. We will all experience suffering, grief, and loss, either individually or in the form of collective trauma. It is just the shadow side of the Yin/Yang price we pay for existence. Everything changes. All change is for a reason and only for a season. As the world we live in changes, we must change too in some way to adapt. The prize does not go to the fastest or the most intelligent. Survival is accomplished by those who are best able to adapt to change. It is not enough to merely survive. We must live a life that is aligned with our unique reason and purpose for being. When one becomes so damaged that life's purpose is forgotten and all sense of self obliterated, as perceived reality flips upside down, we can't live an authentic life holding on to who we once defined ourselves to be. We can't cling to a reality that no longer exists.

With so much focus on identifying and demonizing the characteristics of the "ego" as only something to be exorcised, we must examine our true relationship with the ego. The ego is not our enemy, nor is it our friend. It just is. Owning it is what makes us human. It is the price we pay for existence. We must determine whether or not it is our enemy in all of its manifestations, whether it is the boss of us, and whether hunting and killing it is for our highest good. The Realized Self is the boss. The True Self is not threatened or defined by the ego self. The ego is surrendered at the point of merging with Source. It is not murdered. It is surrendered.

My most recent "Dark Night" experience attacked suddenly, ambush-style. I was still reeling from having just suffered a devastating blow of betrayal and what felt like a great sense of loss. A collision of timelines abruptly changed the subject for me, and for the rest of the world. We went to sleep in one reality and woke up in another … Caught in the clutch of the great reaping of a global pandemic. Now everybody is reeling, looking for a sense of self because the world and everything in it just got redefined. We don't have to hunt and kill the ego. Time is killing it. That is what Time does. It neutralizes or kills the ego, one way or the other. However, this is different, it is compounded by the *collective* experience of an event that causes mass physical and ego death.

That is what changed the subject for me as we all were plunged into the horror story of fighting for our lives against an invisible enemy, struggling to rethink our values and priorities. After this mass ego death and subsequent PTSD (Post Traumatic Stress Disorder), how do we reconstruct our lives and restore our self-esteem? The survival-oriented ego can act like an untrained dog misbehaving. A pet owner generally does not seek to destroy the dog but train the dog. A healthy ego keeps the balance at the point where the two seas meet, the physical form and the Ethereal Essence. The ego is the intersection of Light and matter. Don't kill it. We need it. We are to train it, not allow it to train us.

The out-of-control ego is commonly identified as "Narcissistic Personality Disorder." Another more severe manifestation of similar behavioral patterns is known as "Malignant Egophrenia." It takes over a person like a possession, like a spell, and can become dangerously out of control. With a sense of supremacy and entitlement, it rises up seeking to exalt itself over, and harm others, while lacking genuine substance and authentic self-esteem. This spirit tends to be primarily externally focused. It is concerned with appearance, image, being considered important, being looked up to and envied or admired by others. A healthy ego is internally focused and stable in identity as the True Self, unthreatened by the notion of self-examination.

I don't think many get off of the wheel of this spinning, temporal journey, without the transformational experience sometimes classified as a spiritual awakening, triggered by a Dark Night of the Soul. It can manifest as a crisis that could last moments, days, even years. Some live in its shadows for the rest of their lives. It is important to know when to seek help, and equally important to know how to help ourselves. It is vital to recognize the masked face of ego and how its spirit surges through the main arteries of our lives without invitation. This vile spirit can rise up *anywhere,* among our friends, our family, our co-workers, seeking to extinguish our Light.

Manifestations of this naturally occurring rite of passage are characterized by:

- profound feelings of personal failure, despair, sadness for the world, the future, humanity, and one's own life;
- feelings of worthlessness, not mattering;
- feelings of loss of power, personal will, self-control, self-determination;
- loss of interest in the people, places, and activities that were once a source of pleasure;
- feelings of being "cursed, condemned or sentenced" to suffering in this life;

- feelings that nothing is ever going to change;

- hopelessness, powerlessness;

- alienation of family and friends;

- crisis of faith and Divine Providence;

- sensing an intangible loss that cannot be explained;

- major sleep deprivation, isolation, anti-social behavior;

- shattered sense of reality;

- confusion;

- memory loss;

- dissociative thinking and behavior;

- obsessions with mortality;

- feelings of being completely overwhelmed;

- feeling lost, lacking purpose, searching for meaning in life, longing for an unknown home, unknown family, unknown friends;

- symptoms consistent with P.T.S.D. (Post Traumatic Stress Disorder);

- self-devaluation to the point that it is reasonable to consider this person may be engaged in thoughts of self-harm, harming others, or engaging in self-destructive thoughts and behavior, whether they are or not;

- relinquishing a once familiar, spiritual foundation with nothing to replace it.

Manifestations of associated states of consciousness are:

- *Existential Crisis* – This experience is often masked as various types of depression, or something an adjusted mindset can "fix." It occurs when an individual becomes completely overwhelmed with what they perceive as living a purposeless, valueless, meaningless life. It extends to a troubling level of concern with statements like, "Why am I even here? What is the point? What difference will anything ever make … Ever? I don't want to try anymore. Nothing is ever going to change." Such disparaging communications are red flags and require immediate attention and treatment.

- *Soul Loss/Fragmentation* – Emotionally traumatic events can trigger episodes of what is known as Soul Loss or Fragmentation. When experiencing this dangerous phenomenon, spiritual intervention and healing are required, as well as professional psychological treatment. The experience of such a state of shattered reality can have a devastating impact on a person's life and must be taken seriously. A gifted and trusted Shaman can perform what is commonly known as a Soul Retrieval and may be able to retrieve the broken pieces and restore them to their former state, seamlessly.

- *Ego Death* – "Ego Death" refers to the "complete loss of subjective self-identity." The term is used in various interconnected contexts with related significance in death and rebirth mythology. Ego Death is a stage of self-surrender and transition. It can occur suddenly in the aftermath of a traumatic event that results in severe emotional damage. It can also take an unpredictable length of time to unfold. After the shattering of the psyche of the individual, a Spiritual Emergency can trigger Ego Death, which can manifest as the loss of personal identity, as experienced in Dissociative Disorders that demonstrate as issues with compromised memory, emotional disconnect, identity loss, distorted perception, confused sense of self. It may also be a state of consciousness on the threshold of enlightenment.

- *Kenosis* – Kenosis is a state of consciousness in Christian theology. It references Jesus in the act of 'self-emptying,' making "himself nothing." This state manifests as total submission and surrender to the Divine Will of The God. There are references to comparable states of consciousness in most spiritual/mystical traditions. This state may present with similar manifestations as other states of consciousness that are of concern. It is important to determine the difference.

In meditation practice, any of these feelings and states of consciousness can occur just as intentionally as the conditioned fantasy that, in your darkest hour, there will *always* be someone there for you. However, the sensations associated with the experience of the transcendent state known as Turiya can present without any effort, ritual, or particular sadhana (spiritual practice) in place. This spontaneous state of consciousness can visit gently, or it can present with extreme drama, even violence, leaving you feeling ripped to shreds. It will not change what happened that caused the disconnect. It doesn't have to. It will not "fix" anything. It will show you that nothing is broken. It will not make the threatening cause of the painful feelings disappear. It will make the *experiencer* disappear, dying to their former "self" … the ego self. After Self-Realization, there is no threat made against the True Self that can prosper. There is no injury that the Realized Self cannot survive. The self that cannot recover is not real. There is something so Divine about us that all we have to do is connect with the Source of Light Energy within ourselves, rise up into it, and merge in Oneness with the Transcendent Light of Divinity.

On that Dark Night, the soul tosses and turns, torn between another try and another cry … Reflecting on the existential nightmare of, "Why am I even here?" "Who am I, really?" This is *not* a common depression. The Soul's Dark Night is not specific to the personal reality of the experiencer. It is generally characterized by all-encompassing philosophical realizations and gloomy epiphanies that lead to unprecedented states of enlightenment. It is not necessarily a state of having "given up." It is a cleansing, a purging, a process of inner transformation of intention, moral integrity, balance, and purification. While this spiritual crisis is usually temporary, its gifts may endure for a long time.

A depression, however, is more a self-centered cluster of ego-based entanglements, colliding with illusory, temporal self-concepts. When a depression ends, not much has really changed, on an essential level. From the Dark Night of the Soul emerges a sovereign life, re-born into the experience of liberation, spiritually awakened to the fact that it is cherished, guided, protected, and loved by the Beloved, Creator of all. A gentle breeze carries the sweet fragrance of dawn's mist into the cocoon of this new being, caressing the faceless face of this beautiful ethereal butterfly that chose to manifest a transformed life and heal the desolation.

The evolution of consciousness, moving from personal, into transpersonal, and transcendent realities, is hard work. Our energetic investment in the ceaseless pursuit of knowledge of the True Self, is respectfully referred to in mystical circles as "The Great Work." Our efforts pay off in priceless gems of ancient wisdom that help us navigate torrential storms and a turbulent sea of innocent tears. Some try to sidestep the effort involved with the Realization of the True Self. That does not stop it from happening. In order to accomplish a state of "ceasing to exist" as ego, one must first accept there is nothing to accomplish. That was the hardest thing to grasp for me. We already are everything we need to be. We are already nothing, as the True Self, the formless awareness. Our suffering is our offering to the Great Spirit of change. Either we tear down the conditioning of former limiting constructs or continue to contribute to our own suffering and the suffering of every life we touch.

There can be no rebirth

without a dark night of the soul,

a total annihilation of all that you believed in

and thought that you were.

~ Hazrat Inayat Khan ~

My personal Dark Night experience was the trigger that initiated my awareness of a state of consciousness I learned was called Turiya. When I was finally able to shake it off, there was a period of "lost" time. I could not determine how much time had passed. I only remember what felt like the incredible violence of those minutes, hours. From the perspective of the Timeless Realm, it was all the same. All Light had been eaten by something in the darkness … in the nowhere, that was now my new home … alone enough to realize I was not alone. Something was there, holding all of what was left of me. A transcendent state of consciousness was triggered and experienced as pure bliss. Something else was there … a clearly Unknowable, Formless Presence intervened in that Dark Night that was sent to destroy me. To comfort me, *Something* pulled an entire Universe of millions of brilliantly twinkling stars snugly around me as a shimmering blanket. There, the pain of a thousand lifetimes was transmuted into the warm glow of ten thousand lifetimes of the most Sacred Love. The one who had dissolved into that experience was not the same one that emerged from it. Imbued with healing Light on the other side of the violent annihilation of the only "me" I knew … I was embraced and absorbed into some secret place of being.

The wound is the place where the Light enters you.

~ Rumi ~

Causes of the Dark Night of the Soul

Events that can cause a fall into such an experience of utter despair:

- A traumatic experience, occurring recently or in the past, or one that threatens to occur in the future;
- A tragic life-changing event;
- A tragic life-changing loss;
- A collective event, not just individual;
- Changes in health and well-being (physical, mental, emotional, and spiritual);
- Changes in economic stability;
- Changes in social status;
- Changes in living environment;
- Surviving tragic events due to Earth changes, environmental events;
- Surviving personal or collective attacks or events;
- Surviving a violent attack or event;
- Changes in the stability of relationship and family;
- Changes in friendships;
- Betrayal;
- Changes in political and cultural environment;
- Experiencing a perceived, sudden, or gradual loss;
- Homelessness;
- Unemployment;
- Unresolved conflict in the subconscious mind;
- Bullying;
- Negative forces (Negative Energy);
- Hyper-dimensional interference;
- Interactions with low vibrational people;
- Deep and extreme abuse.

<u>The Dark Night of the Soul experience may visit when you or someone you know have experienced</u>:

- Personal disaster (car accidents, injury, robbery);
- Environmental disasters, exposure to toxins, noise pollution;
- Combat exposure;
- Substance abuse drama;
- Political and social unrest;
- Disasters due to Earth changes, floods, earthquakes, weather;
- Physical assault;
- Surviving a violent attack;
- Surviving a violent attack by authority figures;
- Childhood emotional/physical/sexual abuse;
- Sexual violence;
- Being threatened, stalked, endangered;
- Being threatened with a weapon;
- Online stalking and/or bullying;
- Diagnosis of an illness;
- Chronic illness;
- Issues relating to death and mortality;
- Addiction;
- Empty nest syndrome;
- Parental narcissistic abuse;
- Narcissistic abuse may also occur in adult/adult relationships with its recipes for predictable cycles and scenarios of Love-bombing/Idolization, Manipulation, Gas Lighting, Blaming, Devaluation, Humiliation, Attack/Rescue scenarios, Rage, Sabotage, Silent treatment, Betrayals of trust, Triangulation drama, Debasing projections;
- Pressure and stress at work;
- Anxiety of workload pressure;
- Anxiety of academic workload pressure;

- Overwhelming family duties;
- Caring for an ill or aging family member;
- Divorce;
- Custody Battles;
- Loss of, or changes in employment;
- Financial hardship;
- Being a perfectionist and competing with self and others;
- Being a control freak and feeling out of control;
- Hopeless or pessimistic outlook on life;
- Lack of sound, uninterrupted sleep;
- Lack of social support circle, family, friends;
- Lack of healthy coping mechanisms or engaging in unhealthy ones;
- Untreated mental illness;
- Unfulfilling career goals;
- Problematic energy with coworkers;
- Major depression;
- Anxiety disorder;
- Social anxiety;
- Mood disorder;
- Lacking spiritual support structures.

Be aware and concerned when events occur with no apparent cause that may indicate a *Spiritual Emergency*:

- Unusual and extreme emotional states;
- Extreme depression;
- Thoughts of self-harm or harming others;
- Family, friends, pets behaving in uncharacteristic ways;
- Increase in the exchange of negative energy, arguments, violence;
- Unusual, recurrent, chronic illnesses with no apparent cause;

- Unusual changes in the frequency of, or occurrence of accidents, and/or mishaps;
- Hyper-dimensional interference, flashes of light and/or shadows with no apparent source;
- Strange infestations or unusual appearance of insects;
- Unexplainable sounds with no apparent source;
- Cigar, cigarette smells with no apparent cause;
- Events occur that defy logic and coincidence;
- Bizarre microclimates in the home or around the person;
- Strange weather events;
- Electrical appliances malfunctioning in unusual ways;
- Technical devices malfunctioning in unusual ways;
- Autonomous complex;
- Unexplained confusion regarding perceptions of God and Its antithesis;
- A disconnect from the world and everyone in it.

The cyclical nature of life, with its twists and turns, ups and downs, and ins and outs, can mimic a haunting in the transitional phases of a cycle's beginning or ending. *OR*, perhaps the Universe is intervening on behalf of the higher good of all concerned. *OR*, perhaps it is the Will of Divine Intervention and mandates Destiny. *OR*, maybe it is all of the above. According to Buddhist philosophy, the naturally occurring experience of all life, The Three Marks of Existence, can land us in the experience of the Dark Night of the Soul. It is not personal. The Universe is not picking on any of us. Everything and everyone will *Change*, *Suffer*, and *Return* to our State of Origin. There is no way to avoid it. It is the price we pay for existence.

God

I searched for God and found only myself.
I searched for myself and found only God.

~ Rumi ~

The word "God" is a concept, a term used so loosely that in most of its casual expressions, it is indistinguishable from a social media emoji, or an acronym called OMG. My references to God as "The God" in this text transcend the realm of conceptual religiosity and points to That which cannot be named, but is the Author of all names; That which cannot be painted in pictures, but is the Author of all images and forms, including our own; That which cannot be confined within the walls of divisive concepts, or formed as a weapon by creation, to use against creation, with declarations of judgment, conflict, and control. References to the fact that there exists *Something* beyond known reality, among all languages, cultures, and traditions that reminds us that we did not create ourselves. In deep enough states of meditation and prayer, that *Something* that exists in the Realms beyond "The Unknowable" … has "touched" many who believed in nothing … just to be known. One Touch reveals the State of the True Self … Light merging with Light. That ONEness … with That Beloved ONE … That Beloved ONE of shared Essence.

So many people are caused angst for being battle weary from the drama that so often accompanies the mention of the word "God." Such a symbol of comfort and Ultimate Transcendence has been reduced to a judgment, a battle cry, a declaration of war, a weapon of soul destruction, or distraction at best … a relinquishment of personal responsibility for one's own spiritually sovereign life.

I do not seek to offend anyone. I don't seek to be perceived as spiritually ambiguous, or inclusive for the sake of marketable "correctness." I stand in that placeless place, *beyond* the judgment of mere mortals, like myself. I seek to *surrender* the "self" that can be named; the self I can see morphing in my mirrors; the small acceptance-seeking self, so full of worldly wants and desires. I surrender to the Light that fearful, broken self that others can scrutinize and paint with vile, subjective critique and judgment while demanding that I conform to *their* personal reality. As that caricature is surrendered, a Higher Self emerges, as a brilliant Light of Divine Essence, as a State of Grace … *beyond* the hellish worlds of names and forms.

The meaning of the word "God" and its many translations are subjective. It is important to me that I be clear on who and what I am talking about when I use the word in this text. If you are submerged in a Dark Night experience, and with the voice of duality begin calling on the Universe, the Absolute, the White Light … *anyone* could show up, including Lucifer, whose name literally translates as Light. I believe that neither of these characterizations in this play of polar opposites are personifications. A famous Tesla quote communicates, "If you want to find the secrets of the Universe, think in terms of Energy, Frequency, and Vibration." That is how I imagine The God in Its Formlessness … Energy, Frequency, and Vibration, be it Light or Shadow. Both Light and Shadow energies rise up, even in the eyes of our best friends, in the emotions of our relationships, in the hearts of our families, in the mirrors of our judgments … especially the judgments we make against our own selves. From the perspective of primordial existence, beyond us, beyond language, beyond rhetoric, beyond Time, there is simply a deeper conversation to be had.

We must be specific in what is relevant to our own reality. For example; This is the English version of SELFLESS. I speak English. I will say "God" but not necessarily referring to The God of any particular religion's perspective, or the people who practice it. When the Spanish version of this book is released, it will make references to "Dios" … but not necessarily the "Dios" of any particular religion or person practicing it. When I say "God," I am not referring to a pantheon of deities or embodiments of attributes and energies. If it has a name, that means someone or something named it. What is named is *not* the Absolute Source. What, and who named it would be the Absolute Source. It is Nameless. When I make references to The Deity, I AM speaking of the Creator and Sustainer of all things. I AM speaking with the voiceless voice of shared Essence, and have no perception of separateness from That which is the Eternal Flame of this individuated spark called "me." I AM speaking of the UNKNOWABLE, on the level of my highest understanding and personal experience of It.

When the Light of our common, limited knowledge has been sucked out of our lives, which is something we will all experience, we must call *specifically* on That Which Created all. The understanding of how it is uttered is important too. Consider this, what if something happens to our physical vocal cords that casts us into a mute, silent condition? A Dark Night of the Soul experience is capable of triggering such a state, if only as a temporary episode. *Then*, How do we … Who do we "call" out to for help? We must reach back beyond language, into the Original Breath, that First Breath before it is ever taken, for our answers. We must see beyond the duality of good/bad, right/wrong, darkness/light in our judgments of and opinions of the manifestations of Divine Will. We may not always understand, as we melt into the despairing energy of WHY? We cannot fathom the reasoning of The God, we are human, the God is not a human. Even if we don't believe there is anything there, a Dark Night experience can make us test that, even with no name or form in mind. In such a moment, the Unknowable is fully capable of making Itself known and manifest.

There is a longing specific to those moments, that can feel as though it will last forever. Whatever we choose to call upon externally, know that its Essence is also within our own being. Our power is realized by connecting into the Source of all connections … as if there could be a moment when it wasn't. Let the voice of our deepest surrender call from the point of our most profound longing for connection with the Ultimate Light. As we feel that spark and Flame unite, we rise into the silence of the Dark Night and prepare to embrace the dawn … SELFLESS.

The Unknowable is:

- Pure, Timeless, Unchanging, Formless, Genderless, Distinctionless Consciousness;
- Ultimate Reality, The Highest Universal Principle;
- The Ultimate Cause of all that exists;
- The Infinite, Pervasive, The Unchanging Eternal Truth and Bliss, yet The Cause of all that changes;
- The Creative Principle, The Permanent, Unaffected, Absolute, Highest Reality;
- The Interconnected Spiritual Oneness in all of created existence;
- The Unlimited, Self-Born, Innately Sovereign, and Free;
- The Absence of duality;
- The Universal Soul inside of each being;
- The Universal Soul outside of each being;
- The Origin and The End of all things, physical and nonphysical;
- All souls, all of existence, across all Time and Space, are One and the same;
- There is no individual soul, nor a separate Unlimited Cosmic Soul;
- The Author of Compassion for creation;
- The Limitless One, The Universal Inner Harmony, The Root, The Source of all there is.

Realization of the relationship between The God Essence and creation:

- Something beyond our imagination appeared out of the darkness … A Divine Energy within Light … within matter;

23

- We all have an inherent awareness of the inner presence of the Spirit of Divinity. That is the Essence of who we are. That is our Light. We can experience It with senses we did not know existed. Our True Purpose is revealed by whatever means the connection is made. Forgetfulness of our True Purpose causes our Light to fade. Losing hope causes our Light to fade. Allowing the depletion of our Life Force and positive energy causes our Light to fade;

- It cannot be understood by rational or logical reasoning. It can be best known by all human beings through our Sacred Journey within;

- When the brilliant Light of our True Self becomes obscured by ignorance and false identities, we are not able to witness the inner Light of our own Divinity;

- We put ourselves in boxes and label ourselves. There are mystical techniques that can enable us to take off the labels, open the box, look inside, and determine the True Identity of who or what is actually there. When false identity is removed, the True Self is realized;

- The Original Essence of The Creator (Source) is not an externalized, *separate* entity. It is within each of us, within all creatures, within all things, existing in Oneness with Source;

- The knowledge of The God is attained by Self-Inquiry;

- Knowing our True Self is realizing our Sacred Relationship with The God on the most Essential level of our Being;

- The True Self can neither fall into fear nor suffer damage;

- Suffering falls away when one becomes conscious of the Truth of our Oneness with The God, at that point seeing the True Self in all beings, and all beings in the True Self;

- We are released from suffering when we accept responsibility for our relationship with *all* of creation … *everything* … *all* beings, and *all* of nature, as the I AM, the True Self. It rises up in the *formerly* self-conscious being as empathy and compassion for the well-being of others;

- The Sacred Longing is an expression of the desire for 'Connection' or Oneness with Source, and it will never stop. The Longing *is* the 'Connection' ... the Oneness.

One is One. One is One. One is One. One is One. One is One. One is One.

Let There be Light

Two Wings of the Same Bird

Two Wings of the Same Bird

The Dark Night of the Soul

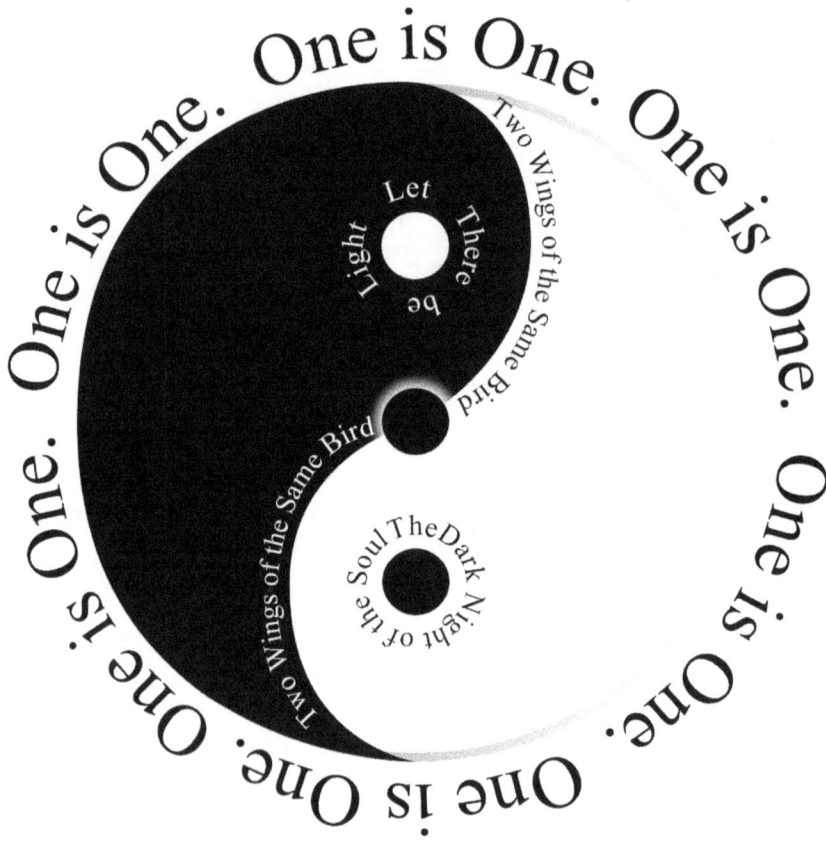

The Study of this Though-Form Cluster is a Powerful Meditation.

The Three Marks of Existence

Change does not care what we believe in. The Three Marks of Existence, according to Buddhist philosophy, address our conditioning regarding existence and death in times of suffering, loss, and grief. There is profound healing available in understanding that our suffering is not personal, just a reality of life. Anicca is just one of the Three Marks of Existence. I would be remiss to reference one and not the other two Laws. They are essentially connected.

This is not a book about religion. It is a sharing of philosophies and secular meditation practices that, in my time of need, offered a profound healing after the devastating loss of my mother. Death and grief drift in the Ether of our being as a counsel and advisor, independent of our beliefs and opinions. Many religions and belief systems have spawned philosophies that have gone mainstream in diverse cultures around the world. Many contemporary traditions have roots in age-old mystical practices. We accept this medicine of the ancient mystics and healers with love and gratitude.

All things are characterized by the Three Marks of Existence. The First Mark or Law of existence is Change … the Impermanence doctrine or Anicca. According to the Law of Impermanence, human life embodies the fluidity of change in the aging process, the cycles of birth and rebirth, and in the experience of loss. The Buddha declared that "Decay is inherent in all component things." His followers accept that conditioned phenomena can also be referred to as compounded, constructed, or fabricated. This is in contrast to the unconditioned, uncompounded, and unfabricated Nirvana. Nirvana is the reality that knows no change, decline, or death. Anything that is temporary is an illusion. All that is true reality is that which is not subject to change and does not come and go. We affirm that only the unchanging is real.

The Second Mark or Law of Existence is suffering or Dukkha, unsatisfactoriness, or unhappiness. As great as this gift of temporal life is, we cannot and will not enter and exit this plane of existence without experiencing pain, loss, and suffering. This phenomenal field of our own perception offers no illusion of a pain-free worldly experience. It is characterized by Impermanence, and some form of suffering or Dukkha is the result of that. The Law of Dukkha is characteristic of the human condition, and here unsatisfactoriness manifests as the kind of suffering we experience when we lose a loved one or wrestle with our fears regarding the transience of our own existence.

The Third Mark or Law of Existence is Anatta or no-self, no-thing. It is the ultimate unfolding of the annihilation of the ego. It is the ego that clings with attachment to being defined by conditioned concepts and identities structured around the physical form. I have heard the "True Self" described as a metaphorical drop of water released into a vast sea. The drop of water is not diminished by merging with the sea, an entity of the same element as itself. Though it may seem that some of the self-hood of the drop of water was sacrificed, it is actually expanded as it becomes one with the vastness of the sea. It moves beyond the distinguishable boundaries of its expression as a form called a "drop" with no loss of identity. It is water, as much as it ever was. We are much like that drop of water, with our self-imposed boundaries, limitations, labels, and superficial identifications. As our subtlest level of Self releases into the vastness of the Origin of all there is, we merge and realize we have only become That which our True Self was, in essence, all along … The I AM.

The experience of union with the Divine dissolves the ego, and it becomes empty of the desire for individuated existence, unattached to personhood, becoming the Oneness with Ultimate Conscious Awareness. Becoming reabsorbed into the Point of our Divine Origin is the most exalted state of becoming One with the Ultimate in the realm of the Incomprehensible … the Unfathomable … the Unknowable … beyond language and names, as no-thing.

As we meditate on the Divinity of the True Self, the realization of "Self," as such, can cause the ego to feel threatened. It can feel like we are disappearing. To conquer the urge to drift back into delusion and perpetual suffering is to taste freedom and experience liberation. Entertaining the false illusions of the ego self is a powerful human instinct and one of the most potent sources of ignorance and pain. There is more than one way to transcend the bondage of suffering associated with the changes of inevitable impermanence. The dissolving of the ego triggers an awakening to the true nature of the transcendent Self. The revelation of a Timeless, stateless state leads to the unveiling of our relationship with the Divine, as One with That Holy Essence ... In the Self-Illuminating Triple Darkness of Negative Existence. We are the reed flute, and the Beloved is the Breath that becomes our Life Force.

Our Attachment to Maya (Illusory Material World)

One does not casually fall into a Dark Night of the Soul experience. When we find ourselves lost in the abyss, something or someone triggered the fall. Something or someone pushed us there. It could be an unfortunate fate, a hard lesson learned, or it could be Destiny pushing us to our highest good. Nothing is as compelling as a Divinely decreed transformation whose Time has come. Whether or not it was an individual or a collective, the same question must be asked, "What are we doing with our daylight?"

Are we clutching and clinging to the illusions and comfort zones of Maya, ignoring the whispers as they turn into shouts. The answer to that question will address the reasoning behind the visitation of the Dark Night. Is it visiting just to get our attention and show us the other side of the veil, so that we may understand Ultimate Reality? Is this transcendent experience an initiatory right of passage? Could it be that Our True Destiny magnetized us to attract it at some point in our lives? Is it Dukkha (pain, loss, and suffering), one of the Three Marks of Existence, the shadow side of the Light of Life?

Maya (The Illusory Material World):

- Maya refers to the Physical Realm of Existence;
- Maya is conscious of the purpose it was meant to serve;
- Maya is the Effect; The Divine One is the Cause;
- Maya is temporal. It is bound by Time and Space under Universal Law. It is Impermanent. It is born, evolves, and dies;
- Maya is the illusory, temporary, changeful, perceived, and transient reality;
- Maya is the collective of all of the emanatory possibilities from The Ultimate Origin of Cause, as a seed contains a tree;

- The physical body vehicle is of the Realm of Maya. It should not be viewed through the lens of duality or judgment. Human existence is not made less by its transience. It is not born as corruption, fraudulence, evil, weakness, or unqualified as creation, just for the fact that it is perishable. It elegantly cloaks its formlessness with the garment of perishable being, brutally tried by its fragile qualities. It is the test that turns to testimony of its Eternal nature and Oneness with the Divine One. It is a sign, faultless in its fragility, compassion, and goodness in its presence as the True Self. Its liberation is experienced in the Realization of the True Self and the knowledge that it is Eternal;

- The knowledge of the Divinity of our True Self, results in the perfect, Timeless unification of our soul with That of The God, the souls of everyone, everything, and all of creation. The peak of the individual's human experience is not focused only on an afterlife/past-life/future-life context. It is refocused instead upon pure consciousness in the *present* life occurring only in The Now, as Time is circular, not linear;

- Our complete absorption into the Energy of Divinity seals our Self-Realization as a brilliant spark of consciousness from That Divine Flame. It is secure enough, loving enough, to give us the freedom to make mistakes by granting us Free Will. It is non-dual, not good or bad, not safe or dangerous, not creative or destructive … no either/or scenarios. It is All. Our challenge is learning how to evolve spiritually and become One with It. As that spark becomes one with the Flame, our sacred surrender will guide us to use our Light for the sake of the entire collective, and become a catalyst for change, ascending to realities higher than the angels.

- The Realization of the True Self and the shedding of the natural attachment to Maya removes suffering, misery, sorrow, and grief from a *person's* life. The dropping of the false identities of personhood allows for clearer knowledge, distinguishing the difference between that which comes and goes and that which is permanent. All that is permanent is That Point of Origin. At the point of realization of the True Self, the "person" releases attachments to the transient.

The person seeks, desires, and longs only for the experience as the True Self, and not the illusion of the body/mind identification displayed in our mirrors.

I do not recommend that anyone deliberately induce a Dark Night of the Soul experience merely for the sake of triggering any meditative state, including Turiya. I do recommend that it be studied for its relevance to the rites of passage on the Journey of our Soul.

Maya: The Archetype, is an excerpt from, FACELESS: THE SACRED RELATIONSHIP, our advanced manual for Archetypal Meditation.

Maya: The Archetype

When her shadow called out to me, I did not answer. When she tempted my senses to attachment and aversion with skillful seduction, I did not succumb. I sought refuge in the Light of my own sacred relationship with Divinity when she struck out at me; when she attempted to destroy me for my indifference; for my rejection of her trappings. Rather than choosing to hate Maya, I chose to surrender in Love for The God of all sides of the veils between worlds. I accepted the Divine purpose of Maya. Rather than curse her mischievous manipulations, I chose to increase my praise for the Wisdom of The God of all creation. I chose to bask in the Light of The Divine One, as a spark of The Eternal Essence, unconditionally ... Without judgment, not lamenting the appearance of shadows.

Profile of Maya's Cyclical Archetypal Influence

The material world incessantly beckons and calls, whispers and screams, baits and switches. Some call her Dunya. Some call her Maya. Some call her Babylon. She is a beautiful seductress, powerful and unwavering. Her ambition is to have us live in her shadows, sell our souls for her superficial trappings, and bow at her clay feet. Her victory is our forgetfulness of who we really are, as we lower ourselves to live for, and as the external, rather than the Eternal. She is a major archetype of humanity. We cannot escape her encounters. We prayerfully break her bewitching spell with ceaseless reminders that she is around every corner we turn, even as we turn within.

Maya is a term found in Pali and Sanskrit literature that has many meanings. Here it means a constantly changing appearance that is unreal, an illusion, or delusion. Maya represents the limited perception of a purely physical and mental, linear existence. The manifestation of the many forms and faces of Maya's illusions causes us great resistance and struggle with our desire for it to be a reality. Her illusions extend beyond the manifest worlds to include our perceptions of self. Our minds naturally seek to construct a fixed reality around the image of "self" that we see in the mirror, even as it changes with our every breath. That we are real, in that context, only constitutes a truth, but certainly not *the* truth. We are more than what we can see. There is something about us that time cannot touch, and it is our blessing to pursue the most profound depths of the knowledge of what that is. The I AM, that cosmic spirit that we truly are beneath the veil of the "I" that we can see cries out to be known and loved.

Maya is a dream the Creator shares with us. We are the dreamers, and we are the dream in this elaborate play on the stage where thought-form becomes form, and sensation whispers to us of its reality until we believe it to be true. As we believe it to be true, we begin to identify with all we perceive of this beautiful and dangerous illusion. Fickle threads of ego-consciousness and karma become braided into our being as a gripping force that seduces us into the energies of craving, clinging, attachment, and begging the *temporal* for *forever*. We have this body for transportation on this Sacred journey. Why do we spin so much energy around the desire for its permanence and ignore that part of ourselves that is Timeless? This is the binding energy of Maya, the dream that awakens to the embodiment of creation … The mind of humanity forming the connecting link between consciousness and matter.

Maya is the full Moon's reflection shimmering on still water. Maya is the glistening of bubbles that rise with an appearance of form for the moments of their brief dance, even as they ascend into their own forgetfulness as they pass away. Maya is the subtle drama of rainbows and mist, neither real nor unreal, not feeling vulnerable to time and impermanence. We must become like waves prancing across the sea of its own element, unafraid for their individuated existence, upon their reunion with Source. We awaken from the dream world of Maya as a being of Light, not fearing past or future, not disappearing, but bursting into the flames of enlightenment that reduce our masks to ashes, exposing the formless face of the Timeless Now.

Death looms overhead in clouds that threaten a downpour of painful loss and separation from the worldly, perishable things and states that we have become attached to. Death becomes the enemy of our being rather than the door to our home of eternal being. We cringe and bemoan it. We cry and we loathe it. We break as we hear the footsteps of the inevitable as they draw near our door, knowing that all of these emotions are reasonable, and our denial is futile. Still believing, somewhere on the highest level of our deepest knowing that *we do not die*. We are Timeless.

Strip Maya down of her stories and scripts, her props and promises, her flirtatious wink of the eye, cloaking the secret of her formidable relationship with Time. Time will consume all things, but the Timeless, even the curtain that appears to open and close between acts and shows, resting comfortably in the consciousness of the Timeless Now, with no attachment, no aversion … No ego.

In the mystic teachings of the Vedanta tradition, Maya is the realm of phenomena that dares us to transcend it and expose it as the hypnosis of a "dream" that manifested as creation. It is a Divine drama played out on a stage constructed by thought-forms, desire, and passion. Maya is neither friend nor enemy. She is both. We, in all of our glorious array of decorated forms and images, are the many manifestations of the Divine One, individuated and identified as we see fit. To know this fundamental truth is to pierce the veil of Maya and see the Source of its emanation. To pierce her veil is to free ourselves from the ever-revolving wheel of life and death, in its circular continuum, from this Karmic, merry-go-round, and roller-coaster existence.

Our objective is to rise above the tendency of assigning permanent qualities to the transient reality of Maya, the material realm of manifestation. She appears to resist the Law of Impermanence at times, luring us under her powerful spell. We are pulled into a web of conceptual misunderstanding. It is a mirage so beautiful, with images so convincing that we are invested in tricking ourselves into thinking it is real. Our ego-consciousness craves these sultry manipulations. With such a tight grip on what is tangible, therefore believable, profound fear of the most natural transition is born … The fear of death. We fear Impermanence as a curse, even though we know it operates within the authority realm of Divine Order.

We are stitched securely in our garments of personhood, bound tightly in the straitjacket of ego identification. We bow down to phenomena, concept, precept, and restless ambition. We are driven by carnal desire and conditioning. We must choose to rise up, focused on Ultimate Truth and Ultimate Reality, that cannot be diminished by labels, judgments, or educated opinion. We are required to raise our frequency to intuit the most fundamental of Universal Truths, defying descriptions based on language for one-dimensional minds to manipulate.

There exists only "*That*" … and "*not That.*" "*That*" is the Unknowable Cause of all things; the Creator; the Unattainable "*That*," the reality of which, we are just a tiny fragment. All that is "*not That*" is Maya. Maya is an emanation of "*That*," willed into existence as ourselves, and all we know. Our goal is to strive to live from pure consciousness, our I AM consciousness. We will free ourselves from our attachment to small manifestations of Ultimate reality, and declare our quest for Self-Realization as One with "That." Everything is One with "*That.*" We are more than the temporal images we see in the mirrors of our minds, with their earthly concerns, possessions, and duality. There is no more small context I, me, my, mine. There are no conceptual dualities such as above and below, good and evil, past and future. We are called to free ourselves from misinterpretations of Self and others. We are liberated as we release our attachment to dualistic thinking, an either "this" or "that" psychological conditioning. That is our encouraged meditation.

The fruit of the unholy tree of bondage to the love of the perishable world is born over-ripe and inspires hunger more than it does satisfaction. The well-woven webs of Maya can ground our attention in the lower frequencies of lower energies, stunting our spiritual growth. The insatiable appetite and greed associated with distortions of Maya ultimately consume all who bow to their soul-seizing compulsions. The aggressive pursuit of flesh and spirit to violate, dominate, enslave, possess, and kill, devours the souls of the weary and weak.

As an archetypal influence, the hypnotic, nebulous realm of Maya is one of the most misunderstood. We may be tangled in its intricate web of manipulations, without conscious awareness that we chose it. It is important to witness ourselves, rather than judge ourselves, as we grow in the understanding that it is *personal*. As long as we see ourselves only as a "person" and not an Eternal being, we are vulnerable to every manner of separation anxiety, while Maya, with her elaborate illusions, has no choice but to ultimately, respectfully, concede to the Law of Impermanence.

The energetic field and frequency, the plane of existence called Maya, is a dream that The God is dreaming. As Maya is the temporal illusion on the material plane, the Sanskrit term *Leela* is the stage in her theater of dreams. This Divine play, with its characteristic dualities, with its pain and pleasure, is the stage upon which our dance with personhood is choreographed. As long as we seek to assign permanent reality to anything in the domain of transient form, we will suffer. We will experience clinging, craving, and yearning for the fantasy. This dance with form and manifestation is why we are here, each with our own unique role to play. The worship of the frills and trappings of Maya can distract and overwhelm the strongest of us, drawing our attention into irreverent obsessions and compulsions. When we awaken from this collective dream time spell, we remember who we really are and spin like a Dervish back into the welcoming arms of The Beloved, our Creator.

Though Maya is demonized by many, this archetype is not solely characterized as the antagonist mindset in an ongoing battle between the forces of good and evil. The energy of Maya manifests as characteristics within our own being, many we are unaware of. Some are hidden from us until the moment someone or something pushes just the right button, at just the right time, in just the right way, opening a floodgate through which our inner demons or angels are released. Even in our resistance to the insidious lower desires of carnal existence, it is no coincidence that our inner demons are the *same* as those we seek to expose and judge in the closets of other people.

An unhealthy attachment to Maya is a form of encapsulated spiritual psychosis. Maya can inspire unwholesome and futile emotional clinging to the world of matter, placing it above eternal reality. This obsession tips the scale of balance into the danger zone of worshiping the trappings of what we call success as a god form. The covetous love of money, material possessions, and physical form can then become the root of all evil. This energy can range from superficiality and greed to soul-selling, unspeakable wickedness. It is an element of the human condition, to the extent that none of us can say we are too perfect to fall under its influence. We continually battle against our own animalistic nature and insatiable desire to maintain our balance. Human desire is like a graveyard … There's always room for one more. The shadow side of our nature is characterized as an ambitious and merciless creature. We are loved by The God that knows we are not perfect and knows how difficult it is for us to keep the balance of Spirit and clay. It is not perfection that is required of us. All that is required is remembrance. If we remember the Love of the Divine One in all that we do, there would be many things that would not even occur to us to do.

Maya knows. Her Third-Eye is wide open, scanning the distance for the next challenge, the next victim, her next playmate. Maya delivers a strong message and warning, carrying with it both a blessing and a curse. Her energy seeks blind satisfaction and immediate gratification. She does not know that there are natural boundaries that must be respected. Some, we are instinctively aware of, while others are taught through cultural conditioning, institutional programming, and the experience of suffering as the result of our choices. Regardless of the urgency of our desires, we are admonished to respect the civilized boundaries of our own higher standards or be delivered painful consequences in self-created cause and effect scenarios. We pray for the strength and the spiritual discernment required to resist the stronghold of the shrewd temptation to forget who we really are.

As we become aware of the captivity of our own minds and desperately try to escape from the slavery of our attachment to worldly ideals, Maya smiles, amused by our conflict of interests. She lures us into her energy with promises of happiness and fulfillment. She whispers the soul slaying lie of "forever 21." Lives and spirits are broken by the effect of the causes created by placing real value on appearances and the illusions of transient things.

We must acknowledge that in keeping with Universal Law, there exists in the shadows the Yang side of creation. There cannot be Light without the casting of shadows, and the Universe will always keep the perfect balance. Where there is excess on either side of that scale of balance, adjustment is built in, whispered between the letters of its spelling. Just as sweet as the taste for creation is the taste for destruction. Those who experience the wrath of this balancing act could easily feel they have been welcomed into hell. We must never feel safe to minimize the destructive potential of Universal Law, operating in the Karmic balance of life. This is an issue of perspective. If we have fallen into the rabbit hole of the illusions of Maya, we have invited the energy of her shadow attributes into our lives. These invitations can be as subtle as the secret thoughts and dreams we keep, or our most coveted fantasies seeking fulfillment. Powerful spiritual strongholds and manipulative thought-forms draw the attention of forces that promise satisfaction, usually at the expense and suffering of others. There is always a price to pay or a reward delivered to our doorstep, either misery or joy, based on the choices we make.

Reminiscent of Steven King's movie, Needful Things, this degenerative process begins with the things we feel we need. Thoughts like, "If I just had the perfect house, car, girl, guy, bank account balance, career, or whatever ... Then I would be happy." This list may go on forever. The material possessions become as obsolete as a typewriter, and yet the hoarding and clutching, grasping, coveting, and clinging never ends. "If I just had another one, or two more, or the one I had in the beginning, or the one my friend has, or the state-of-the-art version I saw on TV ... then I would be happy." Happy never comes, or it comes as a fleeting moment, and costs our eternal soul. None of the things we seek to possess and think we love so much will ever love us back! Much is to be said for ambition. But remember the Biblical passage, "For what is a man profited, if he shall gain the whole world, and lose his soul? Or what shall a man give in exchange for his soul?" (Matthew - 16:26) The Bible (KJV)

Regarding relationships, Maya is a sign forewarning us to embrace the soul satisfaction of a *higher* love ... Love that transcends the body, the mind, even the emotions, seeking the union of two souls. It warns us to seek the abundant Kingdom of The God, which provides for us and protects us. We are not to covet the transient glitter of bargain store soul bartering. At the end of chasing the illusions of matter, we will only find an immense sea of disappointment. We must examine our lives as though our souls depend on it, and cleanse our lives of the belief systems that seek to spoil everything we care about.

It is important within the material realm of being to refrain from playing God in the judgment of others. The energetic domain of Maya rarely defines the totality of anyone's being, regardless of how raw lust, materialism, and greed have eroded a vulnerable character. The energy of Maya is cyclical, for such extremes cause rapid decay and swift ruin. On the other side of what appears to be a rampant free for all, is an epiphany waiting to happen.

In his world-renowned book of poetry, *The Prophet*,
Khalil Gibran said of evil:

Of the good in you I can speak, but not of the evil.
What is evil but good tortured by Its own hunger and thirst?
Verily when good is hungry, it seeks food even in dark caves,
and when it thirsts it drinks even of dead waters.

~ Khalil Gibran ~

The shadow energy of Maya speaks of addiction and perverse obsession, seeking pleasure from that which brings harm to self or others. It advises us to live a more balanced and disciplined life. It also suggests that we have become unbalanced in the neglect of spiritual, creative, and productive pursuits.

There must come a time in life for self-examination to determine if our value systems have faltered in servitude to our egos. We are required to view the world through our Third-Eye, seeing people not as useful carnage, but as spirit. Attachment to the ephemeral can price our souls into Karmic debt and send us tumbling into abysmal hopelessness.

The most important lesson that we could ever hope to learn is that this cartoon-like characterization of a fixed reality is pure theater. Our soul's challenge on this plane of matter is to overcome and survive the animalistic nature of our own human form, and the mischief our minds conjure, even as we sleep. The truth may be difficult to accept. That which causes birth, growth, and renewal, and the Force which destroys, prunes, and reaps are One and the same, the Yin and the Yang.

The magnetism and hypnotism of Maya challenge us to free ourselves from our own cruel and judgmental personalities. We are encouraged to seek and find The God within, with the knowledge that within is also where the bondage of attachment to Maya resides. The greatest holy war of all is the one that is constantly raging within, the conflict between the purity of our Spirit and Essence of our Creator, and the thoughts and desires of the flesh. Our goal is to elevate our thoughts and desires to the level that our souls are the most spiritually comfortable with. A sound, wholesome spiritual practice is the key to maintaining this very delicate balance.

Just as surely as the collective consciousness of high spirituality exists, there is also the collective consciousness of low vibration, worldly desires, and fixations. Our own energy of unbalanced attachment to the temporal world can create a spark that jumps the gap and taps us directly into the stream of energy that we know to be the consciousness of iniquity. This energy can travel through the portals we have created with extremes of grief, anger, rage, hatred, fear, jealousy, lust, loneliness, desperation, and greed. Our subtle bodies, as well as our physical bodies, can become filled with this magnetic negativity, drawing into our lives that energy with which it is resonant. It can feel as though our inner and outer worlds are under siege.

We are born under the influence of the unsleeping and watchful eye of this prevalent, predatory shadow energy. It lies in wait, always poised to jump at the first available opportunity to deliver the next test of our strength of character and mindfulness of what we know to be right and good. When the seductive force of Maya threatens the strength of a firm meditation, it is time to put aside fear and seek refuge in The God of all creation. The most profound protection that can be invoked is accomplished with prayer. Repetitive prayer and chanting of words of power as a mantra can create a vibration capable of expelling internal and external mischievous energies. This practice is a form of prayer, yet, more powerfully, a form of *remaining* in prayer.

My references to the powerful seductions of Maya offer insight regarding the distinctions of her dual nature. While we are given this Divine journey through physical life as a beautiful gift and a lesson, we must never forget the glory of life Eternal in our daily practice. In the soul's depths, our primary defense against the seduction of Maya and its mesmeric, compelling force, is connecting with The Creator through sincere prayer and surrender to Divine Will and Guidance. Only in our binding relationship with The God may our free spirits be lifted up into the realm of the Eternal in the resurrection of our Light. That Union is our firm meditation. Resist extremes. Resist duality. Nothing exists but The God.

Meditation:
The Bridge Between
Worlds of Consciousness

Meditation:

The Bridge Between Worlds of Consciousness

We must know when and how to step out of our own way and venture beyond linear intellect and the consciousness of covetous clinging to a world that is letting us go. The world of the Natural Mystic beckons and offers something that cannot be easily taught. It is not something that needs to be taught, or necessarily sought after. Most of us naturally have a strong resistance to willingly surrendering control of any aspect of our consciousness, that thread of control we think we have over our lives. At some point, even without study and practice, that spark of mysticism that is the nature of our Essence, can auto-ignite the fire of spiritual awakening. A spontaneous event can be triggered that will suddenly break open channels of our consciousness we did not know we possessed. We all have the capacity to experience altered states that are beyond our scope of common understanding. That is what happened to me and confirmed my commitment to strengthening my practice.

The highest goal and objective of this sharing is not to teach or train but to point to the value of an intentional practice to navigate the raging waters of discord that threaten our very existence in the times we are living. These remedies have served well in a timeless context. It is one thing to have a spontaneous mystical meditation experience, absent of hours into years of committed practice toward the goal of achieving it. What I experienced was a gift, far beyond the measure of my investment. It served to show me the practical value of sadhana, along with the importance of pointing it out to others. There is freedom in the knowledge of the mystical sciences that tap the highest potential of self-regulating and choosing the highest frequency of expression of the personal power within ourselves. We become the co-creators of a life experience that reveals the brilliance of the Light of our True Self.

Some make the practice of diverse forms of meditation and study a daily ritual of self-care and maintenance for holistic well-being. *Sadhana*, is a Sanskrit word from the yogic tradition, which means a committed, methodical discipline that includes spiritual exercises that are aimed at maximizing physical, mental, emotional, and spiritual health.

A Sadhana is not limited to one-dimensional concepts of a fitness routine that involves a half-hour of aerobic exercise, opening and closing with a fifteen-minute relaxation meditation. Though it is beneficial, it only skims the surface of the wide range of spiritual healing potential available. A Sadhana aims at achieving perfection in practices that extend to the attainment of Timeless wisdom. This knowledge has the power to transform our daily life experience by using ancient techniques of spiritual/mystical meditative states of consciousness. The intention is to detach from the worldly things that ultimately defeat our most positive efforts. Most traditions practice disciplines toward this objective. The functional expressions of our soundness of practice manifest in the way we think, the way we speak, the way we behave, and the way we treat one another.

It extends to:

- our choices in the way we manage our time in reference to whether or not it is invested in activities which contribute to our physical, mental, spiritual, and emotional growth and development;
- our choices in the company we keep, the conversations we have, the subject matters of focus that dominate our attention;
- the energies and emotions that dominate our intrapersonal relationships;
- the way we manage difficult emotions, conflict, and stressful, challenging situations;
- our capacity to express compassion, empathy, and active concern for the well-being of others;

- our level of tolerance for the influx of discordant energies that exhibit low-frequency, malicious, or violent intent toward self and others;
- our choices in food, entertainment, and recreation;
- the way we breathe and our general posture while sitting, standing, walking.

A Sadhana is not necessarily rigid or exacting in its application. Every personal expression of Sadhana is unique to the practitioner. A practice can be flexible to include any and everything that supports the commitment to optimum health and general well-being.

The least we can expect of a meditation practice is the ability to create the experience of a relaxed and peaceful state of mind, a retreat from the chaos and stress of our lives. Mystical Meditation has been known to trigger unpredictable and often phenomenal experiences. The goal of serious meditation is to quiet the endless, mindless chatter of the ghosts that stalk our subconscious mind. Much of it is self-generated. Some may have visceral experiences that occur much like a lucid dream, with uncanny links to outer reality.

In the practice of meditation, many will enter a semi-trance state and begin to perceive information that is subject to visionary interpretation. To tap into all that is available, we must be fearless enough to journey to the planes of consciousness where dreams occur. These realms are much like our own, parallel to our own, differing in perspective, density, and frequency. The transcendent qualities of the Astral Plane allow that *any* and *every* thing can catalyze the opening of a portal into a deep meditative state, even without our intention to do so. The clouds, the waves upon the water, the sand, rocks, and random stimuli can cause us to be drawn into a meditative trance. There are many ways to accomplish this objective. One of the most effective is to set aside time, if no more than ten to fifteen minutes a day, to dedicate ourselves to a ritual of embracing stillness and silence. Even deeper and more refined realms are attainable through prayer. Sharing the insights revealed in our meditations will serve to become an effective meditation, done in the spirit of prayer. Maintaining a daily journal is encouraged.

There are many subtle techniques that can be used to put ourselves into dream time within moments. For the best results, the practitioner's goal is to experience a shift in perspective about our linear views of Time and Space. This requires a conscious shift of attention from the external to the internal transcendent planes. It requires us to turn within and redefine reality to include dream time, at the crossroads where vertical and horizontal realities meet. In preparation to safely make this shift, we must first draw around ourselves a strong protective force-field of Divine Light with prayer and visualization. This simple but powerful exercise can help to provide an energetic defense shield in a matter of moments with a subtle shift of awareness.

Our most formidable enemy in the assaults against our psyche is the torment of our own fears. To see things as they really are and to see ourselves for who we really are, is the most powerful weapon we have, as long as we remember that the only way to win a war is to not fight it … heal it. With time, it will become a comfortable lifestyle that will provide sound spiritual security, and we will learn more about the costumes and masks of this world.

Important elements of a healthy meditation practice are:

- a handwritten journal;
- good sleeping patterns;
- a healthy diet;
- drinking lots of water;
- regular exercise;
- a sacred space, conducive to comfort, and privacy;

- an environment of like-minded people who respect your practice;
- spending time in nature.

Types of meditation:

- Guided meditation using recorded material;
- Relaxation meditation to manage stress;
- Mindfulness meditation to improve our ability to focus and evolve our thought patterns, "Stone Meditation" by The Dreamcatchers;
- Protection meditation, "Light Meditation" by The Dreamcatchers;
- Mantra meditation;
- Transcendental Meditation (TM);
- Self-Inquiry meditation;
- Transcendent meditation, "Turiya Meditation" by The Dreamcatchers;
- Walking meditation;
- Musical meditation;
- Sound meditation;
- Elemental meditation (air, fire, water, earth, ether);
- Movement meditation therapy such as Tai Chi, Qigong, Yoga, Martial Arts;
- Conscious Ego death, "I Die to My Ego Self Meditation" by the Dreamcatchers;
- Healing meditation to reduce chronic pain, migraines, aid in recovery from injury or illness; treatment of conditions from ADHD to advanced stages of depression;
- Journeying, with or without the use of plant/organic spirit meditation;
- Cleansing, healing, balancing, activation of energy centers of the body;
- Meditation using healing images and focal points;
- Motivational training for job and career efforts to increase productivity;

- Manifestation meditation;
- Visualization meditation.

The symbolic language and imagery of the meditative and dream states unlock the gates to our subconscious mind and spark the intuitive process. A healing takes place in our lives as our conscious awareness connects with our subconscious, uprooting all that our ego has caused us to bury in fear, despair, insecurity, anger, guilt, grief, envy, lust, greed, jealousy, and hatred. It is unearthed, healed, and released. The result is Love, Trust, and the Understanding of our Higher Self as a vital being, connected to the whole of the Universe and The Creator. Our indestructible Hopes and Dreams are the construction materials with which we build the bridge between dreams.

Those who dare may use this bridge to travel back and forth between worlds of consciousness at will and are among the most fortunate of us all. Other worlds coexist in the ethers of our world of matter, on lateral planes, or perhaps we in theirs, so it is not a distant journey. It is innately within our consciousness to be able to find that place. We find that place within … Within the stillness.

The Sacred OM/AUM

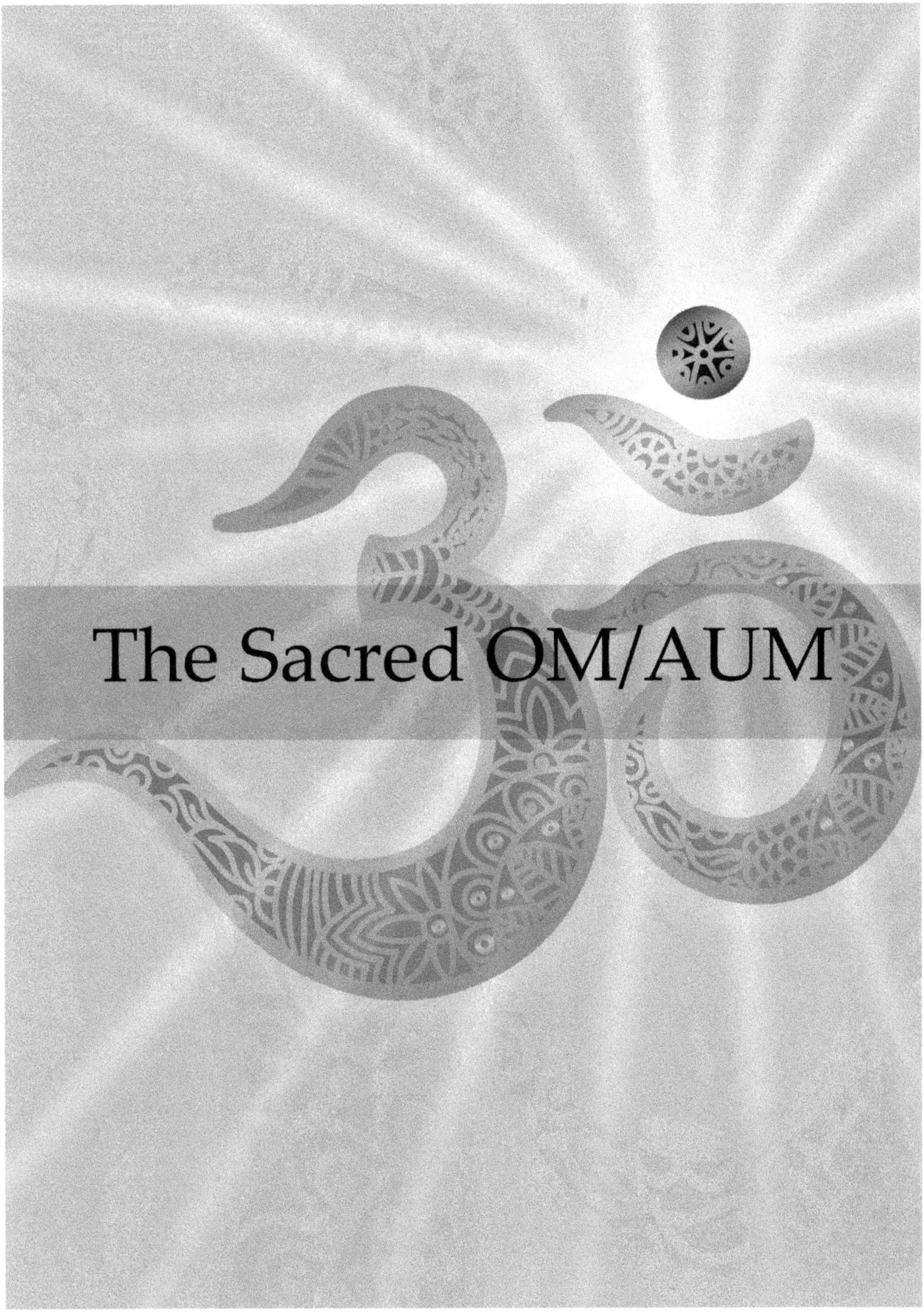

THE SACRED OM/AUM

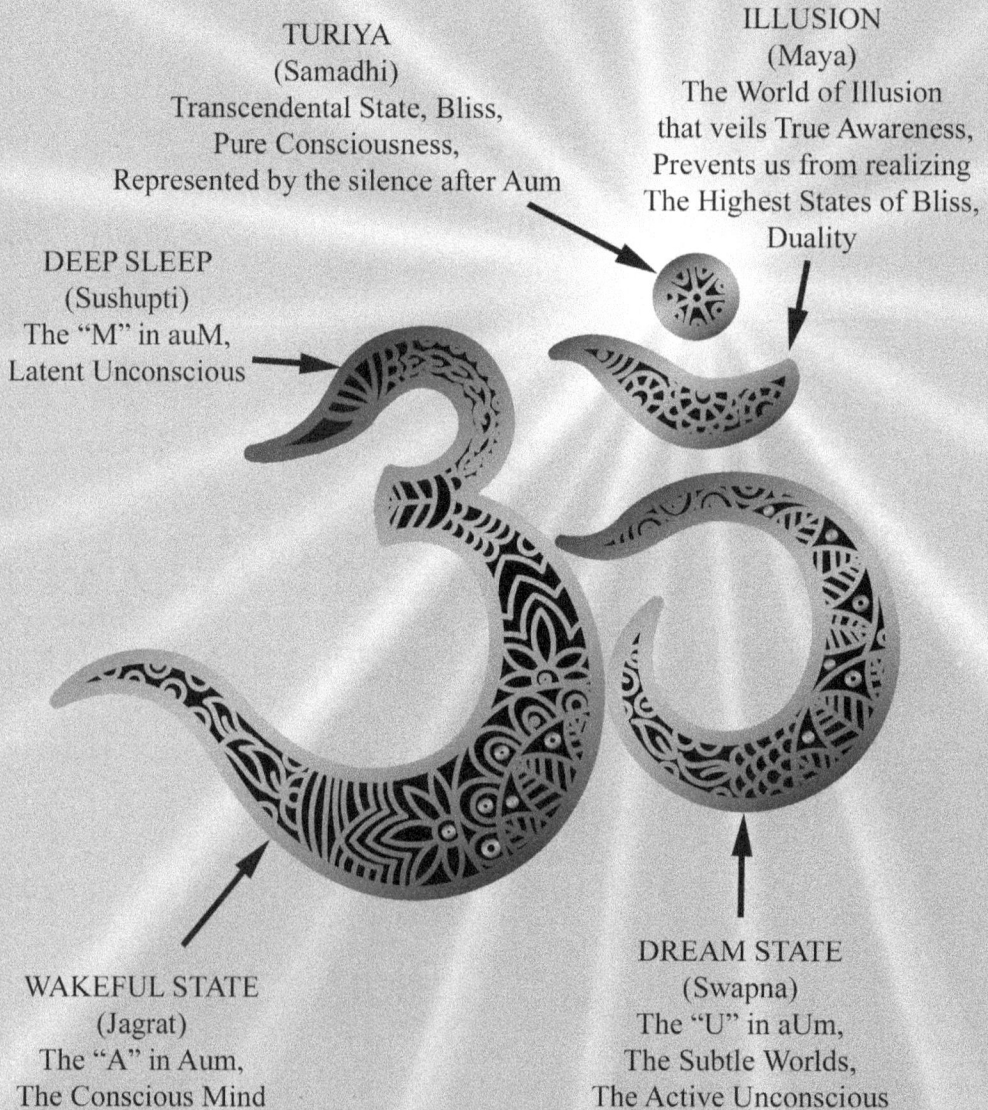

TURIYA
(Samadhi)
Transcendental State, Bliss,
Pure Consciousness,
Represented by the silence after Aum

ILLUSION
(Maya)
The World of Illusion
that veils True Awareness,
Prevents us from realizing
The Highest States of Bliss,
Duality

DEEP SLEEP
(Sushupti)
The "M" in auM,
Latent Unconscious

WAKEFUL STATE
(Jagrat)
The "A" in Aum,
The Conscious Mind

DREAM STATE
(Swapna)
The "U" in aUm,
The Subtle Worlds,
The Active Unconscious

The Meaning of the OM Symbol. 'OM,' 'Ohm,' or 'AUM' is a sacred sound that is known generally as the sound of the Universe. ... The meaning of the OM symbol, while purely looking at its visual form, comes from the states of consciousness that AUM represents.

THE SACRED OM/OHM/AUM

This Ancient Mystical Sanskrit Symbol

represents the original

sound vibration

by which The Creator caused

the Universe to evolve

from chaos to order to creation

and all that sustains it.

It speaks of the dream state,

deep sleep,

the wakeful state,

and the veil of Maya, between them and Turiya.

OM, when intoned with teeth gently touching,

vibrates the skull and the bones of the face

stimulating the Light of

the Third-Eye, at the center of our brow line,

the sixth of our seven energy centers

known as the Chakra System.

The vibration and frequency of the OM

is the sacred connection between the Ultimate I AM

and The Divine manifesting in the I in I,

that Sacred link between Creator

and that which was created.

It is the voice of the Contained calling out

from within the container of our physical form

singing the song of its liberation.

The container can either be a prison

incarcerating our Essence

or it can be the sacred garment

which compliments and adorns It.

The vibration of the OM/AUM,

at the Fifth Chakra

in the area of the throat,

can be the medium

through which It is freed.

Sacred wisdom in wordless Holy language

through the representative visual art

of its evocative calligraphy

can cause the symbol of the OM/AUM

to become a catalytic connection

that seeds the mystical Essence.

This sacred symbol is consistent with the three Sanskrit sounds

A U M representing various fundamental triads believed to be a vibration

of the spoken essence of the Universe.

It is uttered as a mantra

in meditation, affirmations, and blessings.

Let us meditate every day.

We meditate upon The Divine Essence.

Do unto others as we would have them do unto us.

One God

One Love

One Breath

Born of the Eternal OM/AUM

of and into

The Light of the Creator our souls merge

as members of the same body of Eternal Light.

Let us join in this Universal dream.

We will once again

dream together.

Together we will awaken

our lives transformed

to emit our own frequency

and stop living in reference to

and under the influence of

discordant frequencies

that distort our perception of our own reality.

Affirm

I am imperishable.

I choose a life that confirms this truth in every moment.

The Timeless tone of the Sacred OM/AUM is my meditation.

I must never forget who I am.

I remember I am that space

which is shared with no one

but The One

I Am

beyond time

beyond you and me

I am

That

Om

A mantra is a repetition of a sound vibration that produces a centering and healing effect. The Sanskrit word OM (also spelled and enunciated AUM) is one of the most secular and sacred of mantras. It is globally embraced by mystical, spiritual, and philosophical paths as one that can be recited by anyone, regardless of belief system. It is commonly observed as a chant and intonation in yogic (union with the Self) meditations and practices that claim to awaken the Oneness of mind, body, and spirit, leading to enlightenment. The OM symbolizes the original, Source sound of the Creator, and its many variations are generally acknowledged to be a connection to the creative force of all existence. From diverse healing perspectives, the chanting of a powerful mantra is used to cleanse and regenerate the electromagnetic energy field (EMF) for optimum holistic health. The result of this sacred practice, using a mantra (sound), mudra (postures), and breath (Prana/Life Force), is believed to fortify the auric field as a shield of protection from harmful, invading energies and entities.

- AUM registers as four distinct syllables: A, U, M, and that silence of the infinite realm, from which all arises, and into which all dissolves.
- Sound Vibration starts at the FIFTH (throat) CHAKRA, creating a vibration that extends all the way through the CROWN CHAKRA. The energy is moved throughout the body with the proper use of BREATH (Prana).
- *A, intoned in a prolonged "awe" - Waking State*
- *U, intoned in a prolonged "oo" - Dream State*
- *M, intoned (teeth touching) in a prolonged "mmm"- Unconscious State/Deep Sleep*

The Power of Repetitive Prayer

The chanting of mantras and repetitive prayer dates back to the beginning of time. A mantra can be as simple as a single word of power, a vibrational utterance, a childhood prayer. This sacred practice balances and clears internal and external energies, bringing harmony to mind, body, and spirit. The sensation of this powerful energy results in our consciousness being shaken from the perishable realm into Ultimate Reality, the Timeless Now. All healing occurs there where the arrow becomes one with the mark … the Essence … no beginning … no ending … no time … where the prayerful one becomes the prayer.

Words of power in repetitive prayer and chanting can be used for very specific purposes, including the clearing of the dense emotional fog we call grief. The sound and vibration involved with the chanting of mantras can produce transformation and have a positive healing effect. Sacred sounds, repetitive utterances, mantras, chanting, and prayer, date back to the beginning of time. All we know began with the Sacred OM and is sustained by its vibration. It has no energetic beginning or end. It is well worth the effort to study how to engage the power of repetitive prayer, as practiced by so many traditions, on so many spiritual paths. It does not matter what language it is spoken in, as long as it is the language of the very soul of our being.

Repetitive prayer should not be a divisive issue. Among the core mystical groups of most spiritual traditions, the root language is ultimately Sacred Silence. What matters is the breath and the heart's intention, as they are carried upon the magnificent wings of the most surrendered prayer, whispered into the ether. These are not the prayers and chanting of beggars with personal agendas and a list of demands. It is the sound of surrendered fusion with the Absolute Energy and finding the point of connection within. What matters is our ability to suspend our senses and drop all ego self-identification. What counts is how powerfully we are able to withdraw our attention from all distractions and focus it in such a way as to create change on a cellular level. What resonates with, and as Divine, is the purity of our hearts.

The information shared in this book is not meant to be purely remedial. There must be a wholesome, balanced lifestyle in place to support your practice. It makes no sense to have an elaborate altar, consecrated for healing and holistic well-being, if every door to the temple of the soul is swinging open to any, and every, random, sorrowful energy. Much drama would be averted by simply closing and locking the doors in our lives, to the mental and emotional triggers that cause our suffering.

Most paths and traditions practice some form of chanting sacred sounds and words of power, each with their own unique method of repetition. Repetitive prayer is often practiced with a string of a prescribed number of prayer beads, or malas, for counting and focusing attention. There are specific "mudras" or hand and body positions associated with certain systems of chanting, meditations, and prayer. Some are practiced with instrumental accompaniment. Drums bring their own level of vibration and frequency. Some practices include spinning, dancing, or swaying rhythmically, while others require stillness of motion. Your best mantra is the mantra of your choice. The best mantra can be as simple as a childhood prayer, or even as simple as, "Thank You. Thank you for existence." You may feel drawn to a certain mantra or prayer system. Choose with discernment and in-depth knowledge of the meaning of what you are chanting or praying. Repetition of a mantra serves to quiet the over-thinking, reactive mind, inspiring transcendence beyond the origin of thought, into pure awareness. To enter the silence of Ultimate Reality is the goal of most meditation disciplines.

You would be ill-advised to engage in most traditional practices without mindfulness regarding the proper respect for its sacredness, and the strict protocol that must be observed, down to specific subtleties of perfect pronunciation, personal hygiene, and diet. It is worth the effort to study how to perform these very basic but profound healing rituals. This practice is prescribed in times of emotional suffering as a powerful tool for healing. Use that knowledge to empower your practice. The battle between forces of joy and sorrow is a choice and a perception. We are given the understanding that they are interdependent, and neither is "good" or "bad" … they just are. To see it in the context of a pendulum swinging rather than a balance being kept, we become an enemy to our own emotional stability. We may find the worst enemy of our happiness in the mirror. That is where the energetic cleansing begins. Removing the magnets that attract emotional drama will result in a more peaceful life.

One of the simplest of disciplines is the repetitive chanting of "OM." The energy from the vibration engages the Third-Eye and has the power to induce a deep meditative and transcendental state of consciousness, which serves many healing purposes. The Sanskrit symbol for the sacred OM illustrates the four states of consciousness. Our spiritual practice strives for the fourth level, the transcendent state of the Higher Self. From that perspective, healing from emotional trauma is viewed differently. The first question would be, "Who is the 'self/Self' that is suffering?" If the personhood is suffering, the person must be dropped, and the matter must be taken to another realm to be resolved … or dissolved. From a transcendental perspective, there is no "self," consequently, no self to grieve. Once the trappings of the ego self, with its conditioned, subconscious, cultural narratives have been stripped away, the Self that remains knows that it cannot be harmed, damaged, or killed. It knows that it is Timeless, formless, identity-less, label-less, and without agenda or interest in carnal worries rooted in victimhood.

There is no refuge in form

The OM/AUM

The Sacred OM/AUM is the original sound through which the Universe was created and is sustained. It awakens the Light of the Third Eye Chakra .

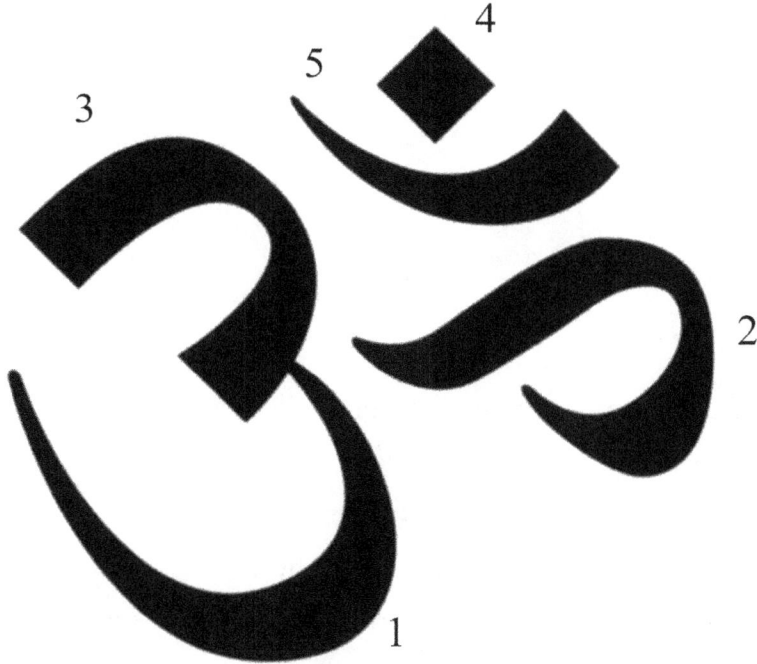

The Four States of Consciousness and the World of Illusion

1. Waking (Jagrat)
2. Dreaming (Swapna)
3. Deep sleep (Sushupti)
4. Transcendental state (Turiya)
5. The world of illusion (Maya)

States of Consciousness of OM/AUM

State 1 – Waking (Jagrat)

- The "A" in OM (A-U-M);
- Conscious Awareness;
- Time/Space Continuum;
- Personal "I";
- Body/Mind Identification;
- External World;
- Covered by the Veil of Maya (Illusory World).

State 2 – Dreaming (Svapna)

- The "U" in OM (A-U-M);
- Still in Time/Space, but mutable, unstable, fluctuating, shifting, changeable, wavering, compared to waking state;
- Inward directed energy, but still under external influences;
- Mind is free to create and experience ethereal realities with quieted senses;
- Parallels waking realities in union of seer/seen, subject/object relationship.

State 3 – Deep Sleep (Susupti)

- The "M" in OM (A-U-M);
- Outside of Time/Space Continuum;
- Outside of body/mind identity consciousness;
- Inside the dreaming of Dreamtime World;
- We are aware of having been in this state only after we have returned to full consciousness;
- The experience of this state is required for our revitalization and to sustain our holistic well-being;
- Undifferentiated awareness, state of deep sleep, unconscious, oblivious.

State 4 – Transcendental (Turiya)

- Experiential knowledge of what the sages identify as Oneness with Divinity;
- The Supreme Consciousness;
- The individuated consciousness merges with The Supreme Consciousness, Source, The God;
- The experience of merging with, or absorption into Pure Consciousness when the experiencer merges with the Absolute;
- It is beyond Time or Space;
- There is no duality;
- It is the *silence* that follows OM (A-U-M);
- It is called The Fourth State;
- The Fourth State is Eternal, unlike the other three states that come and go in it;
- Changeless;
- The direct experience of the Realm of the Absolute;
- It is the underlying, transcendent reality behind all three states of consciousness;
- It is a state of consciousness that extends beyond the context of a meditation practice or experience, and spontaneously presents as a state called "flow" to a quiet mind;
- Turiya is obtainable in Samadhi, and they share many qualities;
- The "Bliss" State is the bliss of the experience of the True Self.

The Turiya State can be induced. It is said that enlightened master, Sri Ramana Maharshi, the Sage of Arunachala, would awaken this transcendent state of consciousness in spiritual seekers through his silent presence and a pensive gaze. It is a common state to experience in some Yoga meditations and practices, in various levels of Samadhi, the yogic deep sleep, thoughtless state of consciousness.

5. The Veil (Maya)

- The world of illusion;
- The world of names and forms;
- The world of masks of false identity;
- Duality;
- Seeks to conceal the True Self;
- Deeply invested in keeping the veil intact, as a desert mirage ceasing to claim attention once it is named, and the True Self revealed.

Beyond States – Turiyatita

Turiyatita is the "Stateless" State, beyond the Fourth State of consciousness called Turiya. As Turiya is the Witness, Turiyatita dissolves into all that is witnessed and all that is beyond witnessing. In the pure Unity of its absorption, it disappears into Oneness with Divinity … The Absolute … beyond form … beyond formlessness … Beyond. Turiyatita is the foundational, pervasive presence behind each of the other states. Each of the States is Impermanent, as they come and they go. Turiya/Turiyatita is the only permanent State …. the only one of them that is real. It is the Ultimate, simultaneously existing Reality of all of the states, as they occur.

Why Use Root or Symbolic Language in Spiritual Practice?

Translations of sacred scriptures are offered in many languages. A wise mystic and spiritual practitioner generally prefer the use of root languages in ritual work because of the potential for confusion using others, particularly English. I assert this, assuming that because this book is in English, the reader speaks or understands English. I am certain that The God will hear and understand our prayers no matter what language we use, as long as we respect and know to Whom that prayer is directed. However, the problem with language can originate in our own subconscious understanding. Our mouths may chant a mantra. Our hands may write a petition. Our minds, our souls, may extend a prayer. Any of these practices used to commune with Spirit may be well understood on a conscious level. At the same time, our subconscious mind may discern subtle, but powerful contradictions between our spirit's deepest desire and an awkwardly expressed intention using a derivative language.

The use of certain root languages, such as Hebrew, Arabic, and Sanskrit, can more clearly express our purest intentions, with the least room for misinterpretation, misdirection, and misunderstanding. Even though confusion may occur in our own minds on a subconscious level, that is where it could be the most compromising to the outcome of our spiritual work. The subconscious mind is the origin of the thought-form from which a strong-willed intention emanates. It may fertilize a corrupted seed through which the fruit of a poison tree is multiplied. When this predictable phenomenon occurs and a thought-form manifests, we can refer back to that original prayer, mantra, meditation, or petition, and examine the corruption in the wording of a derivative language. We don't want to learn the hard way that such misunderstandings can be the root cause of a corrupted manifestation. We may reflect upon the essence of our intention, observe the twisted meanings, braided into the words of our original petition, and discover the source of the corrupted materialization. That is why, when using one of the derivative languages, well-known sayings come to mind, "Be careful what you ask for because you just may get it. No prayer goes unanswered." Our intention and desire must be expressed in pure, concise, specific, and humble perfection for optimum results in our spiritual practice.

There are many factors to be considered. Culture plays its part. Emotion plays its part. Mindset and temperament play a part. However, all of these things are expressed in the *word* and the vibration of the word. When we practice ancient spiritual traditions using a modern language imbued with the understanding from which it rises, tragic mistakes can be made. The other side of that coin is that glorious new energies can be experienced. We do not think like the people of many ancient spiritual traditions. We are often vain in our perception that one culture and one language should reign superior over the entire range of human experience, which is the narrative some traditions appear to perpetuate. There are words from ancient languages that have no English equivalent at all. The study of such words can serve to enhance our experience of life and expand our perceptions. There are mantras that not only have no English equivalent, they can only be expressed using a symbol, sound, symbolic language, tone, or simply silence.

Sound, vibration, tone, silence, breath, and mudra can all be used to create portals into planes of existence and states of being. Mudra in this text is derived from Sanskrit, meaning seal or mystery, and refers to symbolic hand and finger positions, posture, and movement in meditation. Images may do the same thing, yet I recommend caution in their use for the practice of meditation. I won't qualify that in this section because that would be, at the very least, another book. The spark created by intense emotion is the primary causal factor of mystical practice. There are silent meanings infused into language based on tradition, legends, and culturally conditioned phenomena. We use language in such a way as to empower the words or text, which are reliant on subtext or symbolic, unspoken, emotionally charged thought-forms. If we are using English or a similarly confusing language in our spiritual work, we may manifest a confused or unpredictable outcome because of a conflict between conscious text and thought-forms created by a subtext.

There are communications or transmissions made with symbols formed with the hands, silent gestures, even in the projection of an intense gaze that will affect the object of its attention. Most spiritual and mystical traditions acknowledge a phenomenon called the "evil eye," suggesting that energy can be transferred to another through the eyes in such a way as to cause harm to that person. Many traditions acknowledge a mode of speaking that is believed to be a holy language, utterances beyond our known languages, referred to as "speaking in tongues" or Glossolalia. It is associated with intense, transformative experiences and can trigger transmissions of information from the Prophetic Realm that defy explanation. There are as many methods of communicating sacred mystical knowledge and energy as there are people who believe in it.

The interpretations of visions, dreams, symbols, prayers, meditation, energy, and emotion are often culturally influenced. The flash of emotion, the core level stirring of energy, is a requirement to create that spark between visualization in meditation and the manifestation of our intention. Words and emotions connect differently for diverse reasons as they are filtered through our many cultural and linguistic precepts. For example, white is the color of mourning, death, and grief in Chinese tradition. Western beliefs suggest a different subtext, associating black with being a color connected to death, mourning, grief, and sorrow. A bat may portend good fortune in the East and demon spirits in the West. References to magic or the supernatural may suggest science fiction in one culture and be an accepted reality in another.

We can choose to reassign the energies of a conflict between text and subtext. We can accept as our reality the associations we prefer. Emotional experience and reaction are subjective. Two people can speak the same language, come from the same culture, and share a common understanding of what the subtext of one particular word is. The emotional response and associations inspired by *one word* can be completely different. The psyche and spirit can access energies beyond words. There are some energies so complex they are better expressed using symbols, like the Sanskrit symbol of the OM, which represents a sound and vibration used as a meditation mantra. The symbol of the Yin and Yang, among countless others, evokes spiritual energies for which language has no real equivalent. English, particularly, often imposes cultural and ideological belief systems, which shadow spiritual context. The word, the energy, the emotion, the 'symbol,' the spiritual experience, is the alchemy that together causes the whisperings of powerful suggestions that speak to the heart in many ways.

Language in ritual, meditation, and prayer work is an important study and well worth the effort. When we seek sacred connections with The Divine One, the utmost of respect and reverence is required to keep our signal strong and free of static interference.

Turiya

TURIYA

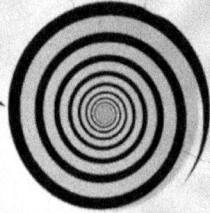

VEIL

OM/AUM

Beyond the Veil of Turiya

Turiya (Sanskrit) is the exalted Fourth State of Pure Consciousness, demonstrated on the diagram of the Sacred Symbol of the OM. The meaning of Turiya is "That which is the Fourth." These "states of consciousness" are often compared to the element of water as it appears in three states, ice, liquid, and steam. Turiya is the most subtle state, so much so that it is arguable that it exists at all. In the State of Turiya, as in each of the other states, there are four states and degrees of subtlety.

We all experience the three states of consciousness, whether or not we are aware of it. These states are not the True Self. The state of the True Self is the witness of all three states with a frequency that starts at the heart and moves up through the Third-Eye. That state is the Fourth State of Turiya. The "Ultimate Self," the state of the "Non-Self," beyond the Fourth State ... Turiyatita. When one finds one's self in the experience of Turiyatita the idea of "Self" disappears, along with the one who witnesses. The one who looks in the mirror at the age of 5 years old and says, "I, Me," and the one who looks in the mirror at the age of 50 years old and says, "I, Me" ... disappears.

From the dawn of time, enlightened beings have savored the unique essence of the Turiya experience, attainable even by the common seeker. There are many names for this coveted, transcendent state of consciousness. Every spiritual practice, religious path, language, and culture has a word to describe the experience of it, especially the language and culture of silence. Nirvana, Samadhi, Satori, Bliss, Spiritual Enlightenment, Fanaa, and others by many other names, are all states of the temporary union of human consciousness with/as Divine Essence. The Fourth State of consciousness, Turiya, smiles just behind the ripped-off veil that separates it from the lower realms of consciousness. At some point, their energies spill over, one into the other, to find that they can peacefully coexist ... The illusory realms of Maya and her maddening, egoic, identity-based consciousness ... and the Unknowable Realms of Divinity.

In Turiya, all that is not our True Self is dissolved as an ice cube dissolves in a warm glass of water. I have heard many Zen/Advaita Meditation Teachers make the "ice cube" reference again and again. I never tire of hearing it, and I use it as a visual meditation/visualization ... The melting of ego ... The Union with the Beloved Divine Presence. That is the ultimate meditation experience, when all that is not who we really are begins to gently melt away, revealing the Light of our True Self. I can't think of a better way to understand the simplicity of the process than that visualization. There are two manifestations of the same element, in different forms, one solid and the other liquid. Under certain conditions, the solid form can change to liquid, and given certain conditions, the liquid form can change to solid, and both could change to vapor. Even if they do not like each other, even if they do not acknowledge one another, that would not change the fact that they are one and the same ... even as they may appear to be different or separate, in different states of being.

Another metaphor, in an attempt to communicate the relationship between associated states of being, is the connection between a wave and an ocean. Does the wave rise up in independence, arrogance, and 'otherness' from the sea? When it falls back into the sea, has it lost, or has it, in some way, failed in its brilliant stand as an independent wave? I don't think so. Nor has it died or in any way ceased to exist. In my experience of being as a wave that dissolved into the sea, I only know what I felt. I only know the fascinating information my research revealed, identifying associated states of human consciousness. The connecting thread between these states is the capability of our personal, apparently solid form to dissolve into the Divine State of Being, in the Realm of the Absolute, and *absolutely* know what The God, The Supreme Consciousness is, in Its Limitless Manifestations. Withdraw attention from the problem. Give the problem to the

Divine Power. In Turiya, there is the awareness that the mind has merged with its Source.

In the Realm of Turiya, all of the vain imaginations of identity and false states of consciousness are dissolved … Even the question of a purpose for being … Even an attachment to, or remembrance of the phenomenon of the experience. It is neither form nor emptiness. All personhood falls away, and the ego-identified "me" experiences itself as the True Self, realizing the purest state of Knowing and Bliss. There, we are free from the desire, aversion, and duality of the illusory world of names and forms.

Turiya is the state-less union with the Realm of the Divine Self. We must not fall into despair over the dissolving, the alchemy of the magical reunion of like elements of Divinity and Its manifestations. We are able to rise into the State of Turiya consciousness to experience liberation and live life as an answered prayer.

Qualities of a Turiya experience:

- Zero-Point Negative Existence;
- No thought … you cannot be attached to anything or anyone;
- Spontaneous detachment;
- Personal stories implode;
- Can occur without prior effort or desire;
- Feeling done with the world;
- Deeper connection to all life, animate and inanimate;
- Sense of indescribable freedom;
- Destabilization of identity;
- Liberation;
- There is a sense of joy for no reason;
- Unconditional compassion;
- You don't have to chase after it;

- You don't return to prior normal states.

Samadhi and Turiya have the same implication, that is awareness of the True Self. However, the surest sign of a relationship between the two states is that so many of the shared qualities are linked by a sense of being the *witness* of all experiences. Beyond Turiya is Turiyatita, the True State of Non-dual awareness. When the nerve centers open up in our brain as four petals of a flower, that is when we can witness what disappears along with the "I," and the "me," and Time and Space.

The Meaning of Union in Turiya

Preparation for this union involves the shedding of layers and layers of attachment, aversion, ego body/mind identification, ignorance, and fear. There is no escape from these false identities, except to know that there is *nothing* to escape. As our consciousness expands to accept the ebb and flow of transcendent realities, we find ourselves beyond this or that, either, or, and all manner of dualistic thinking … and we are free. On our earthly journey, after all of the words … Hope, Light, Truth, even Love … There … NO, *here* in the Silence of the Self-Illuminating, Triple Darkness, is Turiya. The experience of the Realm of Divinity can occur spontaneously and is capable of sparking a full awakening. From Self-Inquiry to Self-Realization, our every moment could be spent in states of transcendent consciousness.

Turiya can be experienced in:

- Waking State as 'Waking-Turiya';
- Dream State;
- Deep Sleep States as 'Sleep-Turiya';
- The State between waking and Sleep States are 'Transitional-Turiya';
- Maya – The Veil of Illusion;
- Waking/Jagrat/physical body/gross;
- Dreaming/Svapia/subtle body;
- Deep Sleep/Sushupti/causal body.

It can descend like a thief in the night or like a cool mist at dawn … But this is no thief, for it bears the gift of Awakening. This is no ordinary mist. It is like the 'cool water misters' in hot climates around shopping malls and sidewalk cafes, but spiked with an energy that triggers subtle states of consciousness that are usually sparked by specific spiritual practices or traumatic experiences. However, such a profound mystical event can, and does, occur spontaneously … experienced as the sense of Unity with the Beloved that Rumi writes about, that the Dervishes whirl into, that churchgoers pray into, that Yogis and Monks meditate into.

I was nowhere and everywhere at the same time. All I could identify of myself, as "self," was energy and pure consciousness, unattached to anything or anyone. I existed as an indistinguishable part of the vastness. There was no darkness or Light, only a Timeless space where the shimmering effervescence and sparkling darkness fused. I felt the personal self of my prior understanding had merged with the Universal Absolute in a Celestial Realm beyond my understanding, where the union of past and future spin into the Eternal Now. I saw everything as *Now*. Everywhere as *Here*. Time and Space were transcended. There was silence and the soundless stillness of a musical vibration of a kitten's purring. It happened in a space beyond prayer … beyond meditation … beyond desire or expectations. It was a blissful state that lasted for hours, that felt like days, that felt like years, that felt like forever.

Something happened that night. I remember losing several hours. I went through the motions I would characterize as "waking up" and announcing to myself, "I'm back." I couldn't figure out where I had been. Out of Body Experiences, Lucid Dreams, and Sleep Paralysis are not strangers to me … even an experience of being "slain in the Spirit" … with no belief system in place to support that anything like that was possible or real. This was different. This was a State beyond all States, unlike anything I had ever experienced. I did nothing. I just lay there trying to figure out what happened. The experience was not initiated by me as any sadhana, spiritual practice, or protocol. There were no mantras chanted, prayers said, spontaneous other-worldly languages spoken. It was a sacred, wordless conversation between creation and Creator in a setting that felt like Zero-Point Negative Existence.

I can't imagine there actually being a "full return" from a state so subtle, so infinite, because such a shift in the perception of consciousness does not return to any former state. I was able to shift back and immediately function in a new norm, present in the localized world and absent to it at the same time, abiding in the unmanifest, non-local as pure awareness … and fully present in the local, mundane … connected only by a cord of breathless breath. I had no go-to practice in place for such an event. I had consciously put aside both a Guided and a Vipassana (Clear Insight) meditation practice, preparing to switch to Metta (Loving Kindness), because I felt I had seen too much.

I am sharing many of the esoteric terms, concepts, and expressions that were once unfamiliar to me, as though I have found the Holy Grail. Much of what has become my lifestyle is not of my tradition or culture of origin. I followed spiritual guidance and resonance that led me to paths of healing through Mystical Meditation. These are only the humble ramblings of someone who is in dedicated pursuit of this redemptive magic. I said from the beginning that I am nobody's teacher, I am an experiencer. I point to things that were pointed out to me. Those pointings worked for me and improved the quality of my life experience. I was just blessed to have been forced to go on a journey of consciousness that would change my life. I took notes. This book represents those "notes." Now I am blessed with the opportunity to share these stories of survival with others, who may be touched and hopefully empowered by them. We will all have something to survive in this life. The sharing of these stories is a sacred healing.

We are time-bound beings who only compromise the true quality of our lives by failing to understand and accept responsibility for the temporal nature of our reality. The only way to win is to strip away all that is not who we really are, and love what is left. Surrender in Love with the Changeless.

The Meaning of Bindi

- In certain spiritual cultures, a Bindi is worn on the forehead, at the focal point of an important energy vortex, the Third-Eye, or Anja Chakra.

- The word Bindi is derived from the Sanskrit word "Bindu," meaning dot or point.

- The Third-Eye is a gateway to higher states of consciousness and Self-Realization.

- The "drop" of Light of all Lights. This Light is not one that is sought for as something outside of the True Self. It is within, seeking Oneness with That which it is already One with. The search is for the realization of that Ultimate Truth.

- In the Sacred OM symbol, the Bindu represents the Turiya State, Absolute Consciousness, the blissful state of silence which comes after the OM.

- It is the realm of Union with the Absolute.

- All things are born from the Bindu and merge back into the Bindu. It is a little dot from which all vast, infinite, and mystical existence begins, is unified with, and returns to.

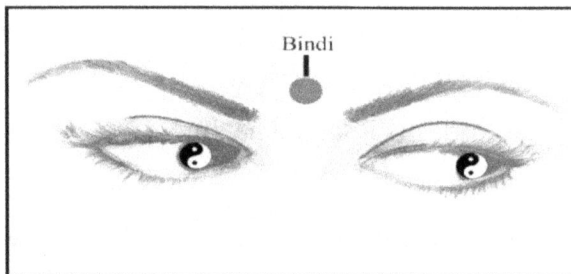

The Bindi is a dot or piece of jewelry placed between the eyebrows and is associated with the Third-Eye. It represents a "drop" of Light from the Ultimate Light, the energies and qualities of Turiya.

"The dark night of the soul comes just before revelation."

~ Joseph Campbell ~

Related States of Consciousness

I have experienced more phenomenal states of consciousness than I *ever* intended to on the meandering paths of my mystical travels. After years of Self-Realization mindfulness meditation practice and study, I fully understood that profoundly dismantling, other-worldly encounters can happen spontaneously of their own accord. An awakening of a dormant consciousness can easily open a portal somewhere between waking and dreaming, piercing the veil between states. It could be triggered by an extremely emotionally charged event, or it could just strike for no apparent reason.

The experience of being catapulted into another dimension by electrically charged energies that spontaneously tapped into my ordinary reality was not unfamiliar to me. I used to say I have always had "trouble staying in my body" because of spontaneous Out of Body Experiences, Astral Projection, Sleep Paralysis, and Lucid Dreaming. My present classification of that type of cross-dimensional drama is that I have always accessed the "witness" consciousness perspective, as a normal or spontaneous state. But this time it was different. What I believe to be an experience of the Turiya State of consciousness, eclipsed them all.

I had not studied the state of consciousness known as Turiya before my experience, and have only just become aware of some of the subtler elements, qualities, and characteristics of its complex manifestations. After extensive research, I documented and meditated on many states of human consciousness with expressions that paralleled what I had experienced. I found many, but the one that resonated the most was the state of Turiya, one of the states of consciousness illustrated in the OM Symbol, that I was already familiar with, as a meditation practice. I just hadn't contemplated the magnitude of the significance of that dot called Turiya on the other side of the veil.

I was not sure if I was slipping into some transcendent state of being or non-being. I felt beyond body/mind state, moving between parallels of Time/Space as total bliss and oneness, into inexplicable freedom ... leading to the direct experience of what I would have to classify as 'non-self.' I either rose or fell into an effervescing formlessness, emerging into realms of Timeless stillness and silence ... some type of void ... as witness, as pure awareness ... luminous senses functioning from another perspective, spontaneous detachment, joy for no reason. There was a sense of not knowing who or what I was. I felt like I was a cloud. I asked myself, was it an encounter with the Infinite, or was it a becoming lost and found in its most beautiful embrace of it?

In the wake of such an experience, there is an echo of the identity of the True Self. The True Self is realized through union and absorption into the Original Essence.

Fulfillment of the criteria for the realization of Turiya:

- Realization of the True Self as the innermost core of Light;
- Realization that the innermost core of the Light of I AM is a spark of the Flame of Divine Consciousness;
- Realization of Union with Divine Source at the circular point of intersection of the vertical and horizontal reality of Oneness in the Realm of Divinity;
- Awakening of the Timeless one who is able to retain that Realization through the experience of all states;
- Becoming the pure State of Turiya;
- Pulling the pure State of Turiya into each realm of life's experiencing ... Self-embodiment.

There are no words to describe the feeling except for having been seized by it. The disintegration of a person's narrow self-concept, social self, and limited intellect ... a drop of water, suddenly aware of being the ocean. The personal "self" is surrendered into the experience of Anatta ... "No Self," one of the Three Marks of Existence. The mystic is now at the point of absorption into the sea of contemplations of Divine Essence. It is beyond the purification and intoxication of spirit. It is the Union with the Divine that Rumi expresses in the ritual of the Whirling Dervishes.

The phenomenally mystical state I found myself swept away into was consistent with descriptions of the Fourth State of Turiya, yet, had elements of each of the states of consciousness I list below.

- *Turiyatita* – Turiyatita is BEYOND Turiya and is *not* only *one* of the states of consciousness, among other states; it is permanent; it is the state of the True Self and permeates *all* of the other states. Interpreted by Sri Ramana Maharshi as a higher perspective of Turiya because only Turiyatita is real; The waking, dreaming, and deep sleep states are unreal because they appear and disappear. The State of Turiyatita is simply BEYOND ... unchanging, non-dual ... the background against which all other states take place ... the True Nature of the True Self ... the state of our True Identity.

- *Samadhi* – Perfect Union of the individualized soul with Infinite Spirit; A State of Oneness; complete absorption. Samadhi, like Turiya, is the realization and experience of the True Self, regardless of the simultaneous experience of other states; There is no sense of "ownership" of anything; As in Turiya, Oneness is experienced in the conscious union of the True Self, the Source of that Spark of Divine Consciousness that we are, and the Absolute.

- *Moksha* – Sanskrit reference to emancipation, liberation, and release from the bondage of Samsara. Samsara is a Sanskrit term that means *wandering*, the world and all of its cyclical changes as it swings in a circular pendulum between concepts of life and death. Moksha is the freedom from ignorance. Moksha is Self-Realization and the extinction of all concepts and identity, and the subsequent state of bliss (Nirvana). It is the cyclical nature of all life, matter, and existence.

- *Fanaa* – (Arabic, Hindi, Urdu: extinction, annihilation, destruction) "Slain in the spirit"; complete absorption into a higher state of consciousness; The highest manifestation of fanaa is reached when the consciousness of having attained fanaa disappears, along with any ego-attachment of recognition for having experienced it; The stage is also called *Fanaa fit Tawheed* (Extinction with the Unity), *Sair illallah* (Extinction of the Self in God) is considered one of the important phases of mystical experience and is attained by the Grace of God, by a traveler on the mystical path; The person becomes extinct in the Will of the Divine One; The Sufis call it "the passing-away of passing-away" (*fanaa al-fanaa*).

- *Sacchidananda* – Sanskrit word referencing the extinction of all concepts and identity and the subsequent State of Bliss, or Nirvana; known by many names, from many different traditions; Satori, Kensho, Moksha, Paradise, Fanaa, Samadhi, Eternal, Timeless bliss or happiness; Transcendent state of consciousness; Shifted identifications from personal body/mind reality to more subtle manifestations of reality; Effects of this experience can manifest in acts of renunciation of harmful actions and behaviors, seeking the release from guilt through sincere repentance, the practice of forgiveness, and total submission to Divine Will.

- *Self-Inquiry* – According to Sri Ramana Maharshi, higher states of consciousness are available with the discovery of and experience of the True Self; The technique of inner inquiry using the thought "Who am I?" to achieve a state of self-witnessing, observing the personal self, and contemplating the nature of the True Self, as the observer; "Ananda (Bliss)" can be experienced after it is determined by Self-Witnessing what one is NOT (Neti Neti – Not this, Not that); True Self-Discovery can yield a direct experience of the Unknowable … the indescribable realm of consciousness and reality of the True Self; Release from suffering caused by neurotic clinging to false identities and narratives; The "awakening" is worth the trauma of experiencing The Dark Night of the Soul … as the questioner disappears.

- *Dhyana* – Sanskrit word meaning contemplation, reflection, sustained attention; Profound, abstract, and mystical paths of meditation; Imaginative vision; Wisdom and reasoning yield incredible mystical power; Dhyana is uninterrupted train of thought; a current of cognition; the flow of awareness.

- *Shunyata/Emptiness/Void* – Emptiness is the antidote for all poisons and defilement of the True Self. Shunyata is the ultimate medicine. It is the medicine that cures the diseases of hatred and anger; The experience of Shunyata is not limited to practice in the settings of a Zendo or Ashram; Does not require a life of renunciation for an energy field suited for this state of consciousness to arise in; It is where "As Above" meets "So Below"; It is the Ultimate Merging of Creator and Creation; To become the authentic experience of Shunyata, one must be egoless and compassionate enough to remain in the Maya (illusory world) with the intention of helping other beings.

- *Yoga Nidra (Sleep Yoga)* – is a meditative state of consciousness between waking and sleeping; This meditation practice is commonly recommended as a remedy for sleep disturbances, particularly insomnia; The body is completely relaxed as the meditator follows a sequence of verbal instructions given by an experienced teacher in a guided meditation; The energetic matrix of the inner consciousness is guided to redirect awareness from a focal point to a conscious withdrawal of the five senses, with the only active sense (hearing) enabled to receive and follow instructions; The experience of Samadhi is common in Yoga Nidra meditation practice.

- *Slain in the Spirit* – This state of consciousness qualifies as a state beyond states; Some of its qualities parallel the Turiya experience; During an experience of being "Slain in the Spirit," the individual is not conscious in an ordinary sense; The transcendent force-field involved has been known to literally knock down a person who has NO belief system to support that it can even happen; "Slain in the Spirit" is a term used by Pentecostal and charismatic Christians to describe this form of prostration; Variations of this phenomenon occur in diverse religious, spiritual, and mystical traditions; It can occur spontaneously at the effect of various triggers, or in some cases, there is no apparent trigger; It is commonly attributed to the power of the Holy Spirit and is an element of faith healing prayer services for illness and spiritual disturbances. This mystifying phenomenon has an electrical quality that invisibly sparks and releases a powerful force which disables the subject on contact; the impact can cause an apparent rewiring of all normal life processes.

The volatile force triggers the energetic extraction of personal qualities and replaces them with an energy so overwhelming, that the person collapses to the floor, exhibiting a total loss of control and in an altered state of consciousness; In some cases, people have been rendered completely unconscious; In some cases, there is notable trembling, crying, shaking, laughing, even violent verbal outbursts, even prophetic transmissions … Each experience is unique; The phenomenon of being "Slain in the Spirit" is not confined to religious events, and has happened under other conditions and circumstances, even as one prays in total seclusion; It is said that when a force with powers attributed to The God contacts human flesh, there *will* be manifestations of its quantum significance in the life of that person.

- *Nirvana* – Transcendent Selfless state, no self, like *Moksha,* beyond the Karmic Time/Space, death/rebirth continuum, salvation, bliss, enlightenment, liberation, freedom from concept, extinction of personhood, release from suffering, perfect peace, most exalted state of consciousness, heavenly state, free of body/mind oriented attachments, desires, and clinging to unreal, transient states and things.

The Fourth Moment

I explore the dance of consciousness
from the non-physical, into the physical realm,
and back again
This sacred dance is Eternal
I share my journey with you
through the worlds within,
where we become the dreams
that are born mature,
the nightmares we can neither forget nor remember
beyond yesterday, today, and forever
There is no past ... The First Moment
There is no future ... The Second Moment
All time is Now ... The Third Moment
In the subtle, spaceless space between them
Beyond Samadhi
In and Out of Time
There is only
The Fourth Moment
The Timeless Now
We embrace this Oneness
with respect, gratitude, and Love.

The process of attempting to understand the Fourth Moment can bring chaos to one's mind. We frustrate our entire being seeking to describe that which cannot be described. How does anyone propose to assign concrete reality to that which transcends the abstract and ethereal in concept? A state of being, so vague, so absent of context, it can only be imagined by comparison to what it is not ... un-nameable, unknowable ... not here-ness, not there-ness ... It is beyond the Three

Moments, Past, Present, and Future. It does not belong to the Now. It is beyond the 'this,' beyond 'that,' something entirely 'else' taking place.

In the wake of the experience of a spontaneous shift from one state of consciousness, into a consciousness with the characteristics described of Turiya, I thought … perhaps it is the Clear Sight vision of Vipassana. But no … In that stateless state there was no seer or seen. I thought … Maybe it is The Fourth Moment, but for it to have been the Fourth Moment, there would have to be other numbers, other Moments, others to experience them … but, no. Wherever, whatever that placeless place was, is beyond numbers or anyone to count them. I felt the Fourth Moment as a still, silent pause of an unexhaled breath that is the threshold between all we know, and all that is Unknowable.

We can only seek to describe the Fourth Moment from a perspective of duality, like sweet/sour, yin/yang, left/right … what it is/what it is not. It is beyond concept and description, beyond words and interpretations. It is a mutual experience. We only *experience* it, without the label of "experience," as it experiences us. We struggle to describe something that does not exist, yet is so real, in a very personal way.

The Fourth Moment cannot materialize itself to be "known." No one can prove it. Inextricably tied to the binding limitations of identity, names, labels, and forms, some may want to struggle to assign it qualities and properties, that we may "understand" it. How does one assign a name to something that does not exist? How does someone seek to describe the indescribable? One can only be in the experience of it, in full awareness of it, in a moment that the next person cannot share, and would be completely oblivious to, even if they were lying beside us as we are experiencing it. The Fourth Moment can only be seen through the eyes/filters of a state of Vipassana (Clear Seeing) Realization, non-egoic consciousness. Past that "seeing" there is Something Else. Past our experience of That … is Oneness with That.

The Fourth Moment is an authentic mystical experience occurring, existing of its own accord, in its own context, its own abstract state … beyond words, beyond explanation, beyond description … without category, which *is* its category. It cannot be considered extraordinary. It is beyond concept, beyond our level of understanding.

Protocol for
Meditation Practice

The Sacred Self

Observe the basic rules of physical and spiritual hygiene when performing meditation and prayer rituals. Some methods include performing ablution, a ritual cleansing as prescribed according to many traditions before spiritual work, and prayer. "Cleanliness is next to Godliness" is not an empty cliché calling out to meaningless ritual. A purification bath of sea salt and baking soda will amply prepare you for intense meditation, cleansing the aura of astral garbage. Soak for about twenty minutes. In the preparation of the bath, as you pray or chant your mantra aloud, run your hands through the water, projecting the energy of your prayers into the water, in a stirring motion. If a tub is not available, make a solution in a separate container or a spray bottle to use in the shower.

Anoint a white candle with olive oil and prayer. Place the candle in a fire-safe location that is easy to view from the tub to provide a pleasant ambiance and a powerful focal point for concentration. Certain oils enhance this cleansing ritual, such as rosemary, rose, and lavender. Engage in your choice of affirmations, visualization, intense prayer, or guided meditation. Do not use a recording of a guided meditation unless you have listened to it first, in its entirety, in a fully conscious state. Determine that you completely understand and are in agreement with every single word of the meditation.

Many read or chant verses from Holy Scriptures. Some engage in prayers that take on the form of personal conversations with The God, with the understanding, that is exactly what they are. I have experienced a quickening of frequency and energy when I ran a slow stream of water from the shower while meditating in the tub. The cleansing of the aura and sacred workspace to prepare for meditation and prayer is accomplished by "smudging," using smoke charged with prayer and positive intention as a clearing of discordant energies. You can burn a "smudge stick" of sage or burn cedar, sweetgrass, Palo Santo, or

Frankincense and Myrrh. Light your sage wand, in prayer, and fan the smoke with your hand or feathers, using your right hand. Pay specific attention to the top of the head (Crown Chakra), Third-Eye or Sixth Chakra (between and just above the brow line), the nape of the neck, the throat, the heart, and the Solar Plexus area, all the way to the bottom of the feet and back up to the Crown Chakra. The smoke represents the rising of the spirit of the prayer to the Great Spirit, the Creator, for spiritual cleansing and protection.

This ritual cleansing should be performed in a manner consistent with your chosen tradition of prayer while visualizing the aura being cleansed of negative energies. In addition to cleansing yourself, take the time to cleanse your meditation area and the entire house with frankincense, myrrh, sweet grass, salt, lime, lavender, and sage, and in some cases Ammonia, prior to spiritual work. What you use, when, how, and why will become intuitive choices as you delve deeper into your studies.

The Importance of Prayer, Intervention, and Faith

I will never advise that meditation is a more effective practice in the recovery process than prayer. Prayer is when you talk to God. Meditation is when you listen. After the trauma of the Dark Night of the Soul phenomenon, you are not prepared to listen to anything but the broken record of your nightmares.

> *He is Eternal, having no birth,*
> *for everyone who has birth will perish.*
> *He is unbegotten, having no beginning;*
> *for everyone who has a beginning has an end.*
> *Since no one rules over him, he has no name,*
> *for whoever has a name is the creation of another.*
>
> *~ The Upanishads ~*

Every prayer is heard. Every prayer is answered. Sometimes the answer is no. Sometimes the silence is a test of faith. In the silence, you may hear the answer spoken to your soul in your own inner voice.

> *I have learned*
> *so much from God*
> *that I can no longer*
> *call myself*
> *a Christian, a Hindu, a Muslim,*
> *a Buddhist, a Jew.*
> *The truth has shared*
> *so much of itself with me*
> *that I can no longer call myself*
> *a man, a woman, an angel,*
> *or even a pure Soul.*
> *Love has befriended Hafiz so completely,*
> *it has turned to ash and freed me*

of every concept and image
my mind has ever known.

~ Hafiz ~

It is tough navigating the unpredictable twists and turns on this road called life. It defies natural instinct and reason to adhere to limiting beliefs of fixed conclusions about just how fluid this mystical Universe really is. Nothing is fixed. Our greatest consolation is to know that we are not our own, whether we know and accept it, or not. We are intrinsically connected to The Creator, God, in a union that is so sacred it cannot be named by our lower plane languages and utterances. We are connected in Essence to That Source Consciousness, a Consciousness so unfathomable that it is pure vanity to imagine it is possible to speak Its Holy Name. Prayer should not fall into a category to be debated or argued to dust. The prayers, meditations, and affirmations are our own sovereign choice, based on what makes us feel the strength of our connection. Our essence and That Essence are One.

Our regular affirmations of belief and submission are vital to our spiritual healing in times of feeling frightened or intimidated. If we waver in our belief of the miraculous nature of The God, all we need to do is look in the mirror. When we look into our own eyes for that spark of Light that we are, we know that we are looking at a miracle. Prayer is our way of communicating with The God. We validate our love and appreciation for The God and heal our own souls with every word of every prayer and sacred thought. In our prayers and meditations, we strip away the flesh and bone vessel that contains the spirit we are and bare our immortal soul to The God in communion with That Essence.

If our prayers are but mindless verbal recitation, we cheat ourselves out of the experience and comfort of the sacred relationship we have with The God. The sacredness of our own relationship with Divinity makes it worth the time and effort to respect the ritual process of preparing to experience that consecrated holy union.

It is worth the mindfulness of unplugging from the matrix of this confusion system to plug into a Higher Energy Source, that of the Most High.

It is healing to elevate the intensity of our longing by not just praying but *remaining* in repetitive prayer and chanting. It is well worth the time we allow in our busy lives for a departure from the vanity-based drama of the perishable world to rest our weary souls in the loving embrace of Ultimate Reality. As we accept responsibility for our spiritual journey, we must be mindful of the fact that we are not alone. We are intrinsically connected at the core of our being to the Source of all healing. In the face of relentless pursuit by the spirit of despair, with its never-ending effort to capture and collect our souls for fun, we submit in prayer to the Will of the Most High in thought, action, and deed.

So why do we bother to pursue metaphysical studies and practices? We do it for the same reasons we exercise the muscles of our physical body even though it is born perfect, even in spite of any of our perceived imperfections. Our perfection rests in the Loving Eyes of our Creator and has little to do with our, or anyone's judgments, opinions, criticisms, or comparisons. Still, we naturally feel compelled to exercise, improve, and groom our already perfect vehicle because that inclination is a natural component of our perfection. However, we are not to bow down to the exercise. We bow down only to The Creator, not to the ritual around our practice.

Prayer is a spiritual exercise. Surrender is the spiritual muscle that results. There, in the spirit of that sacred surrender is faith … faith beyond evidence, beyond proof. The prayer must be a meditation of surrender. The meditation must be a prayer of surrender. From the killing fields of raw fear, all we can do is surrender what is left of us, to the only Force capable of facilitating our healing. I do not represent any one religious or spiritual path over another. The prayers and meditations you choose to engage in are entirely up to you. If the energy of your prayer resonates with the energy of your Higher Self, you will feel it and know.

Sometimes the best and most powerful prayer or meditation is simply, "Thank You."

At this point, I will refer you to the first five sections of my book, FEARLESS: PSYCHIC SELF-DEFENSE – Transcend the Fear of Spiritual Warfare (available as a free download at dreamuniversalmedia.com or for purchase (Kindle and Paperback versions available) at Amazon.com); What is Psychic Self-Defense? The Meaning of I AM (also later in this book), Protect the I AM, I AM Consciousness Rising, and The Mystical Path to Self-Realization. After reading these chapters for an understanding of the I AM, return to this chapter and answer the following questions: Now that I have chosen to distinguish my Eternal True Self from the body-identified, impermanent self ... Does the True Self really worry about not being able to defend Itself? The answer is NO! What does the True Self fear? The answer is NOTHING! The I AM, our Essence, who witnesses who we think we are ... What does it fear? The answer is NOTHING!

I will share with you a few of the prayers from many traditions that I found comforting and healing. I encourage you to share prayers that speak to your soul at dreamuniversalmedia.com, to possibly be used in future publications.

Every prayer is heard. Every prayer is answered. Sometimes the answer is no.
Sometimes the silence is a test of faith. In the silence you may hear the answer
spoken to your soul in your own inner voice.

Release Prayer

The Great and Holy Spirit,

Sacred Mother/Father God

the essence of I,___Name___,

am your humble servant

and You are my Beloved

I seek refuge in your Guidance

and surrender my personal will to Thy Will

at this point where the river of my suffering

meets the shoreless ocean

of Your Love,

Compassion and Mercy

At this time, I stand before You

for guidance on this matter

My soul is burdened

My heart is heavy

and still, my faith

and my gratitude

are stronger than my suffering

I release and submit my willfulness

asking Your forgiveness

for every moment of

falling into forgetfulness

that only You are my sustenance, my providence

Our connection is Sacred

Our One and only reality is Our Oneness

I release my attachment to the outcome
I surrender my personal will to Divine Will

Here in the shadow realms of a desolate night
I release and let go as I seek only Your Light
Here in the brokenness of my heart
that beats only for You
that seeks healing only from You
I wait only for You

The Prayer of Life
The Rebuke of Self-Harm and/or Harming Others

I was given the gift of this body to stay in it for as long as it takes
to hear it called back home in its perfect time
My own voice will never make that call
My own voice will never make that call for another

I realize this is not the home of my spirit
I recognize my soul's yearning for its return home
I evoke the awareness that I am already there, in or out of this body
no matter where else I may appear to be

I can die to this world and never leave my body
I can be here Now
while transcending the pain, the sadness, and the grief
while transcending the loneliness and the suffering
while transcending fear and rejection
I am not asking for my burdens to be taken away
I am asking for the fear to be taken away
and be replaced by the strength to bear it

Angels watch over me
I am never left alone
I cannot fail in this dance of destiny
I am here for that
for as long as it takes to know
that I do not need a body to exist
My body needs me to exist
Inside of it I am the transcendence of all materiality

Right Here
Right Now

The Spark that seeded
ItSelf
my True Self Essence
is Imperishable
Eternal
I affirm that there is no such thing as death
I affirm that the True Self cannot die
I affirm that it is not possible to end my life
I affirm that it is not possible to end the life of another
I affirm that my True Self
survives any attempt to erase myself …
survives any attempt to erase another …
acknowledges that there is no "other"
acknowledges that if I hurt someone else
I hurt myself
I give praise and thanks to The Most High
that all non-resonant thought-forms dissolve
into a thought-filled sea
of forgotten horrors

I affirm that if I should succumb to any negative thought-form
and act upon it
I will be forced to witness the fallout
of the suffering my lower self-willed choice has caused

That part of me that
does not change
does not die

KNOWS

that

I AM Eternal

There is no beginning of me

There is no end of me

Not by my hand, nor the hand of any other

Not by fire, air, water, or earth

I Am One with That from which my True Self emerged

I have chosen not to be the witnessed nor the witness

of any form of destruction triggered by my misguided choices

by my tormented emotions,

by my troubled mind,

by my broken spirit,

by my own personal will,

by my own hand

I have chosen

not to have to witness the pain any untimely departure would cause

on this side of Time and the other

I have chosen to love and accept responsibility

for the gift of my life

the Eternal beauty of my True Self

MY LIFE IS SACRED

MY LIFE IS SACRED

MY LIFE IS SACRED

I have the power to reside in the domain of my Higher Self inside of this body

I have the power to transcend the stories, the faces, the masks, the theater

of the lower realms of my consciousness

I give up

I give up approval seeking, comparisons, and people pleasing

I give up imposing impossible, false, soul-selling standards upon myself

I give up force-fitting the vastness of my Self

into the tiny boxes of illusory realities

that have nothing to do with who I really am

I owe no offerings to the false gods of the fake imagery of others

I am not this body

I was here before it happened

I will be here when it is gone

No thing, no person, no opinion, no circumstance

dares to even try to invalidate the beauty

of this life, this breath, this Light, this Love, that I AM

I AM HERE NOW

I AM THAT which I seek

I am One with the Most High Creator Sacred Mother Father God

of my highest understanding

I am a spark of the Original Flame

There is no difference between us

I forgive myself for this thought of separation

I accept this perfect gift

this beautiful container

which is not who I AM

It too is sacred

for it transports my True Self

through this experiencing

I own the power to OWN it.

I share with you these Biblical verses, offered to me by friends that are used as powerful prayers and mantras, even though I believe prayer can be as informal and spontaneous as a conversation with loved ones. The word, the thought, the prayer, the mantra, that reaches out to connect with Divine Presence, reaches in as well. It is only an acknowledgment of the connection that is already there.

23rd Psalm, The Bible (KJV)

The Lord is my shepherd
I shall not want
He maketh me to lie down in green pastures
He leadeth me beside the still waters
He restoreth my soul
He leadeth me in the paths of righteousness
for his name's sake
Yeah though I walk through the valley of the shadow of death
I shall fear no evil for thou art with me
Thy rod and thy staff they comfort me
Thou preparest a table before me
in the presence of mine enemies
Thou anointest my head with oil
My cup runneth over
Surely goodness and mercy shall follow me
all the days of my life
and I will dwell in the house of the Lord
forever.

Psalm 91, The Bible (KJV)

He that dwelleth in the secret place of the Most High shall abide under the shadow of the Almighty.

I will say of the Lord, He is my refuge and my fortress; my God; in him will I trust.

Surely, he shall deliver thee from the snare of the fowler, and from the noisome pestilence.

He shall cover thee with his feathers, and under his wings shalt thou trust; his truth shall be thy shield and buckler.

Thou shalt not be afraid for the terror by night; nor for the arrow that flieth by day.

Nor for the pestilence that walketh in darkness; nor for the destruction that wasteth at noonday.

A thousand shall fall at thy side, and ten thousand at thy right hand; but it shall not come nigh thee.

Only with thine eyes shalt thou behold and see the reward of the wicked.

Because thou hast made the Lord, which is my refuge, even the Most High, thy habitation;

There shall no evil befall thee, neither shall any plague come nigh thy dwelling.

For he shall give his angels charge over thee, to keep thee in all thy ways.

They shall bear thee up in their hands, lest thou dash thy foot against a stone.

Thou shalt tread upon the lion and adder; the young lion and the dragon shalt thou trample under feet.

Because he hath set his love upon me, therefore will I deliver him; I will set him on high, because he hath known my name.

He shall call upon me, and I will answer him; I will be with him in trouble; I will deliver him, and honor him.

With long life will I satisfy him and shew him my salvation.

Meditation Posture

Yoga-Union of Mind, Body, Spirit, seeking Union with the
Divine One

Mudra-Hand gesture that directs the flow of energy to the body
during meditation

Lotus Position-seated (appropriate for you), back straight,
legs crossed, hands resting on knees, palms up, third fingers
and thumbs touching, mindful natural breathing.

Uttarabodhi (Sanskrit) Hand Mudra
*Thumbs touching and index fingers touching (pointed
down), all other fingers intertwined at the Solar
Plexus level.*

. Inspires sense of inner unity and alignment with Divine Source.
. Enlightment, insight, inspiration.
. Calms the mind, reduces stress levels, improves concentration.
. Dispels fear, realization to fear nothing or nobody except God.
. Problem solving, decision making.
. Improves self-confidence, realization of the Higher Self.
. Refreshes the body system and recharges it with energy.
. Shield for the body and from negative forces.

A **"Mala"** is a garland or string of beads that is
symbolically used for meditation, repitition of
mantras and sacred words of power.

106

I share this translation of the Metta Compassion Meditation.

With origins in Eastern traditions, Metta is practiced worldwide.

The Metta (Loving Kindness) Meditation Prayer

- My heart fills with loving kindness. I love myself. May I be happy. May I be well. May I be peaceful. May I be free.

- May all beings in my vicinity be happy. May they be well. May they be peaceful. May they be free.

- May all beings in my city be happy. May they be well. May they be peaceful. May they be free.

- May all beings in my state be happy. May they be well. May they be peaceful. May they be free.

- May all beings in my country be happy. May they be well. May they be peaceful. May they be free.

- May all beings on my continent be happy. May they be well. May they be peaceful. May they be free.

- May all beings in my hemisphere be happy. May they be well. May they be peaceful. May they be free.

- May all beings on planet Earth be happy. May they be well. May they be peaceful. May they be free.

- May my parents be happy. May they be well. May they be peaceful. May they be free.

- May all my friends be happy. May they be well. May they be peaceful. May they be free.

- May all my enemies be happy. May they be well. May they be peaceful. May they be free.

- May all beings in the Universe be happy. May they be well. May they be peaceful. May they be free.

- If I have hurt anyone, knowingly or unknowingly in thought, word or deed, I ask for their forgiveness.

- If anyone has hurt me, knowingly or unknowingly in thought, word or deed, I extend my forgiveness.

- May all beings everywhere, whether near or far, whether known to me or unknown, be happy. May they be well. May they be peaceful. May they be free.

Light Sphere of Protection

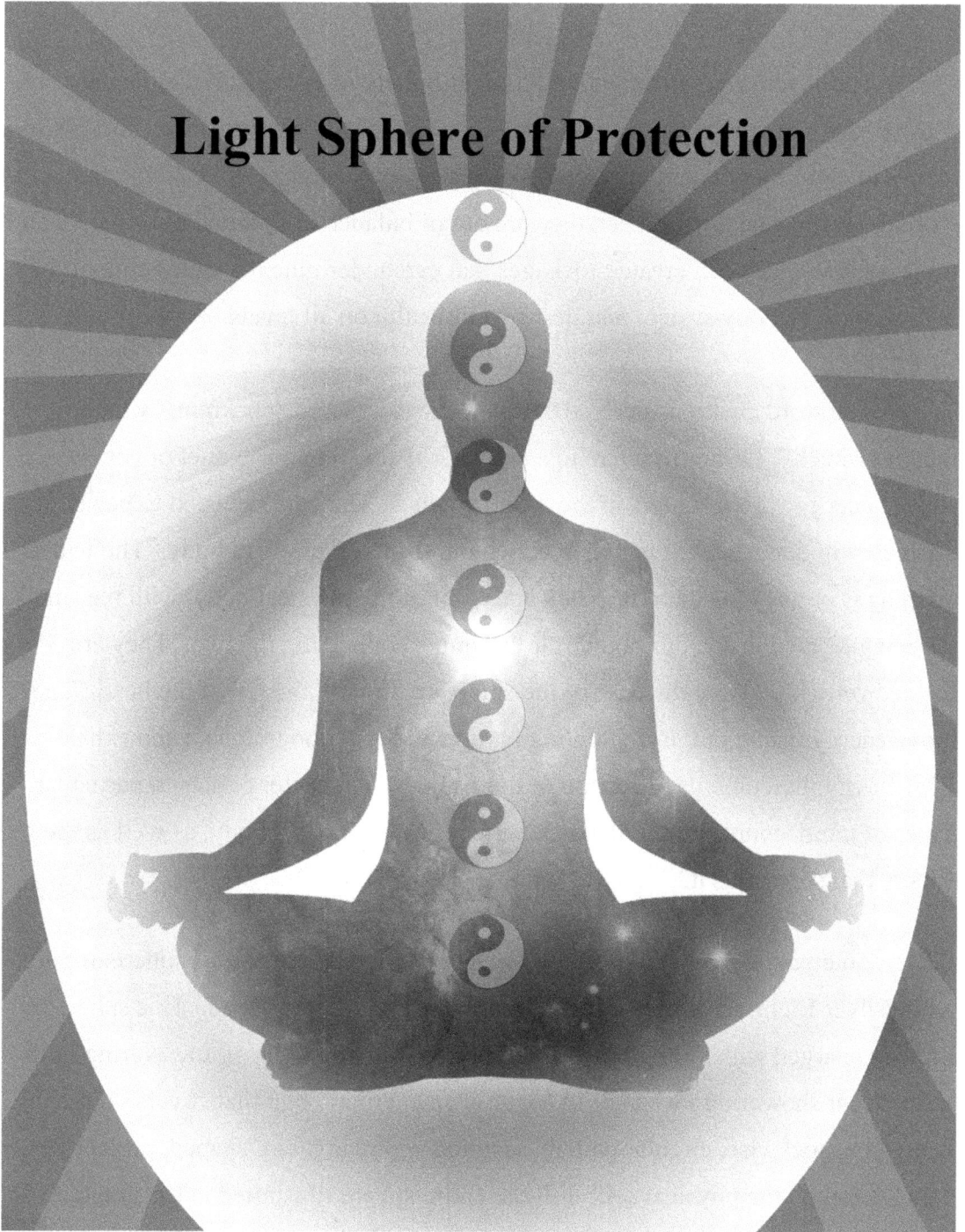

The Light Sphere of Protection

The seven energy centers in the Light Sphere of Protection diagram are illustrated with a Yin Yang symbol that represents the dual nature of creation as it relates to all of these energy centers. When they are energetically healthy, they can work to promote healing. When they are out of balance or polluted by negative and toxic energies, they can create blockages that can undermine the well-being of the entire energetic body system and destroy our health on all levels.

The word chakra is derived from the Sanskrit word "chakram," which means "wheel." This term refers to a network of seven major funnel or cone-shaped energy vortex centers in the "subtle body." They are believed to be about six inches in diameter, extending one inch out from the physical body. The wider opening is on the outside of the back and front of the physical body, with the small tip being located inside our body near the spine, connecting the two. They are located vertically, from the base of the spine, up through the top of the head. They move energy in and out, in a spiraling motion and function to inhale and exhale vital energy, based on the direction of their spin. Each center relates to particular states of mind, connecting to the experiences of the physical body, as well as the energy that surrounds it.

To create a shield of spiritual protection, we will visualize a sphere of pure, white/silver Light, the color of soft lightning just above your head. This sphere of Light is charged with strong prayers and positive affirmations of unwavering faith. Visualize it showering its beautiful Light in an energetic rain that covers your entire being in a clockwise, circular pattern, forming a glowing, egg-shaped, protective aura all around the physical self. Fill the entire sphere illustrated in the graphic with Light. Affirm that no weapon formed against you will prosper.

As we begin to understand the function of the Chakra System and study methods of clearing blockages and cleansing our electromagnetic energy field, we can heal the negative effect on our physical, mental, emotional, and spiritual health. For a more in-depth explanation of the Chakra System, download your free copy of my book FEARLESS: Psychic Self-Defense – Transcend the Fear of Spiritual Warfare at *dreamuniversalmedia.com* or purchase a Kindle or paperback version at *amazon.com*.

This overview will help you perform the most basic of Chakra exercises. See diagrams that follow it. Review the correspondences and select a subject that addresses your issue. Visualize the color in the area of that chakra and affirm its healing. Prayer is the most powerful healer for each chakra. I do not represent any one system of prayer as being more powerful than another. Use prayers offered in this text, along with your own prayers, meditations, and affirmations, to strengthen your own spiritual practice.

Basic Human Chakra System

Chakra/Sanskrit Name		Color/Syllable
Crown Chakra (Sahasrara)	7	Violet/Om
Third Eye Chakra (Ajna)	6	Indigo/Sham
Throat Chakra (Vishuddha)	5	Blue/Hum
Heart Chakra (Anahata)	4	Green/Yam
Solar Plexus Chakra (Manipura)	3	Yellow/Ram
Sacral Chakra (Swadhisthana)	2	Orange/Vam
Root Chakra (Muladhara)	1	Red/Lam

Basic Human Chakra System

Seven Chakra System

Crown Chakra-Violet
Balanced: Connection with Divinity; Portal Between Worlds; Wisdom; Transcendence
Unbalanced: Obsessive; Closed-Mindedness; Greed; Fatigue; Boredom

Third Eye Chakra-Indigo
Balanced: Psychic Eye Vision; Intuition; Truth; Knowledge; Energy; Healing; Compassion
Unbalanced: Poor Concentration; Insomnia; Migraines; Poor Vision; Sinusitus

Throat Chakra-Blue
Balanced: Sense of Hearing; Communication of Truth; Chanting of Mantra;
Purity; Transcend Space/Time
Unbalanced: Poor Communication; Arrogance; Gossip; Secrets;
Lies; Unexpressed Grief; Miscommunication

Heart Chakra-Green
Balanced: Love; Compassion; Empathy; Connection to Divinity; Breath; Joy
Unbalanced: Anger; Jealousy; Betrayal; Grief

Solar Plexus Chakra-Yellow
Balanced: Courage; Confidence; Sovereignity; Self-Esteem; Willpower
Unbalanced: Low Self-Esteem; Trauma; Bi-Directional Criticism

Sacral Chakra-Orange
Balanced: Pleasure; Sexuality; Health and Well-Being;
Creativity; Procreation
Unbalanced: Boundaries; Addictions;
Hyper-Emotionality; Hate; Animalistic Nature

Root Chakra-Red
Balanced: Safety; Security; Power; Birth; Passion
Unbalanced: Materialism; Death; Insecurity; Sexual Obsession

The Chakras

7 - CROWN CHAKRA - VIOLET

- BALANCED: Connection with Divinity; Belief; Wisdom; Understanding; Inner and outer beauty; Pure happiness.

- UNBALANCED: Obsessive attachment; Closed-mindedness; Living in a fantasy; Disconnected from the True Self and reality; Chronic fatigue; Boredom; Greed; Neurological disorders; Migraines.

- HEALING: Prayer; Meditation; Running; Cardio exercises; Yoga.

6 – THIRD-EYE CHAKRA - INDIGO

- BALANCED: Vision; Imagination; Intuition; Truth; Knowledge; Ability to focus; Ability to think clearly and make decisions; Regulates our sleep and waking time.

- UNBALANCED: Rejection of spirituality; Blurred clarity of situations; Poor concentration; Insomnia; Migraines; Sinusitis; Poor vision.

- HEALING: Prayer; Meditation; Relaxation is important; More sleep; Acupuncture; Reiki; Fetal posture or other Yoga poses bending forward; Exercises for the eyes.

5 - THROAT CHAKRA - BLUE

- BALANCED: Hearing and expressing Truth; Throat; Teeth; Neck; Shoulders.

- UNBALANCED: Inability to communicate; Inappropriate communications; Arrogance; Gossip; Secrets.

- HEALING: Prayer; Chanting of Sacred Mantra; Guided meditations; Cleanse energy through singing or sound therapy; Meditation is good therapy to regain confidence and faith.

4 - HEART CHAKRA - GREEN

- BALANCED: Love; Compassion; Connection to Divinity; Bridge between upper and lower Chakras; Seat of the emotions; Breath; Joy; Empathy.

- UNBALANCED: Anger; Jealousy; Betrayal; Grief; Disregard for the humanity of others, Disregard for the sacredness of all beings, all things; Hateful; Spiteful; Unforgiving; Vindictive; Conscienceless; Emotionally unavailable; Detached; Lack of Empathy; Inability to love; Inhumane; Sadistic.

- HEALING: Prayer; Meditation in green environments; Sufi Lataif Meditation; Zen Meditation; Vipassana Meditation; Nyabinghi Drum Meditation.

3 - SOLAR PLEXUS CHAKRA - YELLOW

- BALANCED: Courage; Faith; Confidence; Sovereignty; Sound digestive system; Self-esteem; Willpower.

- UNBALANCED: Trauma, Bi-directional criticism; Low self-esteem; Fear; Lack of faith, No sound spiritual practice or belief system; Vulnerable to entity/spirit interference; Egoic; Arrogance; Extreme manifestations and patterns of narcissistic abuse.

- HEALING: Prayer; Meditation and diet; Surround self with positive energy; Sacred practice (Sadhana).

2 - SACRAL CHAKRA - ORANGE

- BALANCED: Pleasure; Sexuality; Procreation; Identity; Health & Well-being; Positive emotional connections; Creativity.

- UNBALANCED: No boundaries; Obsessions; Addictions; Greed; Envy; Violence.

- HEALING: Prayer; Meditation; Tai Chi; Chi Gong, Aromatherapy; Yoga; Energy healing.

1 - ROOT CHAKRA - RED

- BALANCED: Safety; Security; Power; Birth; Life/Death; Passion; Sexuality; Emotional grounding; Desire; Contentment.

- UNBALANCED: Death; Materialism; Fear; Insecurity; Sexual Obsessions; Violence; Vile behavior; Rage; Cowardice; Disregard for the humanity of others; Bullying; Hatred; Prejudice; Anger management issues; Fiercely competitive; Privileged; Inability to manage life in a grounded way; Inability to get along with others; Inability to take responsibility for actions or behavior; Disregard for consequences; Entitlement.

- HEALING: Prayer; Meditation; Chi Gong; Kundalini Yoga; Bare feet on the ground; Physical activity; Strengthening of the Heart Chakra, Study of Transcendent Spirituality.

Meditation Exercise to Strengthen the Seven Energy Centers

Painful memories and feelings can be trapped in chakra centers for years. Through a committed meditation discipline, these negative energies can be transmuted into pure white Light, illuminating colors corresponding with each chakra, as it is being healed. This spiritual cleansing can change the frequency and raise the vibration of the blocked chakra, in such a way as to repair damage caused by the negative energy that entered. Manifest a powerful healing throughout the entire energetic system with the strength of your intention.

When you responsibly address the life issues that the chakras govern, you will positively affect the optimal health and balance of each chakra. Avoidance of these issues can result in energetic depletion on all levels, and will ultimately manifest as physical, mental, emotional, and spiritual illness.

For example:

The lessons of the First Chakra are those of the physical or material world, issues of survival, self-defense, acquisition, and societal and family, law and order. The First Chakra relates to sexuality, physical desire, ethics, guilt and blame, security and safety, control, and power. These issues, unresolved, will damage that chakra and directly affect the function of the Second through the Seventh or Crown Chakra. Any energy blockage that prevents the flow of the Chi (Life Force) and the gentle rising of the Kundalini energy is detrimental to the entire system. The practice of cleansing the seven energy centers causes a gradual surge upward. It helps your practice to commit to memory, the correspondences, colors, and functions of each chakra.

Meditation Exercise: Ask yourself, "What are the issues relating to the "X" Chakra that I am NOT facing with responsibility?" Make a list of these issues.

Take each issue into meditation after performing cleansing protocol and prayer. Affirm that this condition is being healed at its origin.

After completing your meditation, as with all meditation practices, it is important to ground yourself before you resume your everyday activities, especially before you drive or perform any activity that would require alert, grounded concentration. If you feel light-headed or unfocused after your meditation, there are many ways to ground yourself. Bring yourself back to alertness by washing your face and hands with cold water, eating a serving of fruit, drinking a glass of cool or cold water, walking barefoot on the ground, playing music, dancing, exercising, or taking a brisk walk.

There is a visualization that is commonly used for grounding that works well. Visualize yourself standing with your bare feet planted firmly on the ground or the floor. Imagine yourself sending roots down into the Earth. Inhale through your nose and pull the Earth energy up through your roots. As you exhale, your roots are pushing deeper into the Earth. After several minutes, you will return to your previous state of alertness. At that time, journal your experience and the information you received.

Human Chakra System

Energy of:

Obstructed by:

Realm of Divinity

Ego-based Body/Mind
Identity Attachment

Vision/Intuition

Attachment to Illusion

Truth

Deceit/Hypocrisy

Love

Sorrow/Grief
Heartbreak

Will/Determination

Faithlessness

Desire

Guilt/Remorse

Survival/Existential
Issues

Fear-based
Consciousness

Basic Guidelines for Meditation Practice

Before engaging in any meditation: Observe recommended basic protocol regarding personal hygiene and be attentive to the cleanliness and ambiance of your setting. Sit in a private, quiet, comfortable place with soft lighting, where you will not be disturbed. Assume an erect, comfortable posture. Facing the East is best, energetically. Touch your tongue to the roof of your mouth and clench the buttocks to effectively channel and contain the flow of energy.

Touch your thumbs to the middle fingers of your hands, activating the energies of the planet Jupiter, which attracts good fortune, abundance, and a selfless, charitable, open-minded spirit. This powerful mudra activates the turquoise, blue energy of the Throat Chakra, and the element of sound vibration. It is a medium of verbal and non-verbal expression and communication, even extending into the Etheric Realms. It also effectively contributes to relieving pressure that causes imbalances in the Heart Chakra.

Rest your hands, palms up, on your thighs/knees. If you are not physically able to sit in a full or modified Lotus position, be mindful of your posture and sit up in a comfortable chair. A style of meditation called Yoga Nidra is practiced lying down. There are as many styles and techniques as there are amazing meditation instructors and practitioners.

Prepare a quiet place for prayer and meditation. There should be no television, radio, electronic devices, or distracting conversation. The telephone should be turned off, along with anything else that could startle or disturb you. It is recommended that you remove watches and ticking clocks from your sacred space. Be conscious of excessive exposure to electromagnetic currents for their ability to scramble your frequency.

Keep the lighting warm and avoid fluorescent lights. Avoid meditating in complete darkness and never meditate under fluorescent or CFL (compact fluorescent lighting). They disrupt your auric field, causing it to become disoriented. They produce dead orgone energy that can compromise your immune system, your moods, and make you physically sick. Dead orgone (Universal Life-Force) energy from fluorescent lighting can be blocked by safely using a decorative cloth covering as shading, to lessen exposure to its harmful effects. A single white candle can be a relaxing focal point.

Take particular care in the maintenance of a clean, healthy aura. The human aura can be negatively affected by the energy you expose yourself to. Thoughts are things. We are all being constantly bombarded with negative thought-forms, energies, and vibrations from our environment, as well as the negativity that we generate from within ourselves. The electromagnetic force-field around the physical body requires maintenance to keep it cleansed of the garbage that so easily attaches to it and drains our positive energy. An accumulation of this negative energy can make us walking magnets for bad experiences and compromised health. An unhealthy aura is a breeding ground for spiritual, mental, emotional, and physical disease.

The aura may be cleansed in many ways, including the use of crystals and semi-precious stones, which promote balance and restore positive energy. Proper use of certain types of crystals can improve psychic and spiritual abilities when used in meditation, with the understanding, of course, that the magic is not in the crystals. The magic is within you and your connection with the Divine One. Understand, as well, that this is not trendy jewelry. If you are not prepared to study and practice the proper care and maintenance of crystals and other sacred meditation tools, it is best just to leave them alone. A whole book can be written about how to respect their sacred energy. Spiritual cleansing baths, meditation, and prayer are powerful purification practices for the personal self and sacred paraphernalia.

Be mindful of your breathing. Use your breath as a focal point in your meditations. As a way of staying focused and raising your vibration, the chanting of a mantra that is sacred to you helps to facilitate cleansing and protection. Be mindful of the mantra that you choose to chant. Make sure that if it is in a language that you do not understand, get the literal translation and study it before beginning your practice. I have witnessed people chanting up their worst nightmares because of a misguided meditation practice and a carelessly chosen mantra. One of the greatest mantras is simply *Thank You.* Chant it and become conscious gratitude, living under Ultimate Grace. I do not recommend any particular mudra (hand, finger, posture positions) to perform the meditations in this book. It is worth the effort to research and experiment with the mudras that are best for your preferred system of meditation. It is not a cursory study, but it is a rewarding one that is certainly worth the effort.

Don't eat, drink, smoke, chew gum, or participate in idle chatter when engaged in spiritual work. This behavior is distracting and vulgar. You are cultivating your ability to focus and concentrate, and you do not want to engage in gross and disruptive behaviors. That does not show a proper level of respect for yourself or the sacredness of spiritual practice. These guidelines fall under the category of common manners.

No alcohol or drugs. Do not ingest any substance that would alter your consciousness before, during, or after meditating. This absolutely includes consciousness-altering pharmaceutical drugs. Consult with the medical practitioner who prescribed your medication and ask if there are risks that are relevant to a meditation practice. Any substance that causes impairment can attract energies and entities that are better left crouching in the distance, far, far away. Depending upon the depth of your trance or dream state, there are times during sleep and meditation when you are as pure conscious awareness, drifting out of the physical body. That is risky enough without adding intoxicants that distort the effect and experience of meditation. It can result in adding increased and dangerous detachment between the physical and non-physical bodies.

Meditating while intoxicated is as dangerous as driving drunk. You may provide a willing host for some random discarnate being, wandering through the lower Astral planes, anxious to seize a form to occupy, as you drift out of a drunk or drugged body. It may not even be personal. In this book, I have precisely documented my research, however, what I share is mostly based on decades of personal experience.

Do not meditate under the influence of any form of intoxicant! Even after meditation, it is not wise to fall under the influence of any intoxicating substance. You may not be grounded enough to maintain complete control of your energies.

It is not advisable to go into deep meditation on a full stomach. There are no hard and fast rules on this one. Eating a heavy meal before meditation and spiritual practice inhibits the ability to focus and concentrate because of our grounded energy. A full stomach can dull the senses and interfere with the discernment of subtle communications.

Take a question into meditation. Never go into a meditation without a prayer or acknowledgment of resonance with the Realm of Divinity and a spirit of gratitude and humility. Given certain necessary conditions, you can spontaneously tap into a current of Timeless information, Past, Present, and Future, that can direct and assist you in life. Listen for guidance.

Evoke the protective White Light of Divine Spirit to envelop the essence of every manifestation of your being. The deepest and most profound meditations are entered into in a prayerful state of mind. The feeling of safety and security will enable you to relax, knowing that you are cloaked in Divine protection. Know that the Light that protects us is the Light that we are. We emanated from that Light.

Hold all information revealed in a Mystical Meditation in strict confidence, especially if it relates to someone else. Never reveal information you have received relating to someone else to anyone other than the person that it involves. It is a spiritual violation. It is as unethical as a medical doctor or therapist betraying the confidence of a patient by disclosing personal information shared in consultation.

Never diagnose an illness, or recommend treatment even if the information you have received in a meditation reveals information that indicates there is a problem. Heed messages and warnings, and then consult a trusted medical professional. Do not be an alarmist. You can *create* illness and disease in your mind and body if you are not careful about the interpretation of what is perceived to be negative information. A fear-based interpretation can result in life-harming choices. Use discretion. It is dangerous, as well as illegal, to diagnose or recommend treatment for an illness in such a way as to practice medicine if you intuit information for others in your meditations or dreams.

It is best to avoid meditation when tired, sick, angry, extremely depressed, or in a general state of extreme fatigue. Your unstable, ungrounded energy may compromise your meditation experience. Remember that gloomy moods can alter the quality of your meditation. In such a case, it would be advisable to pray your strongest prayer before entering into a meditative state.

Journal changes in your sleep patterns. This is not Law, but you may notice your dream patterns changing as you begin to open the doors of forgotten chambers of your subconscious mind through meditation. Studying and practicing a discipline of meditation will trigger spontaneous releases of transcendent memory, connecting you to other frequencies and realities. The act of meditating is so powerfully charged with cosmic energy that welcome or unwelcome drama may become attracted to your dreamtime world. Many tried and true, ancient and modern practices will keep you in charge of the company you keep, whether you are awake, asleep, or during meditation.

<u>A Note of Caution:</u>

The studies in this text are for informational purposes only and not intended to diagnose, treat, cure, or prevent any disease. If you are experiencing symptoms of diagnosed or undiagnosed emotional or mental illness, clinical depression, thoughts of harming yourself or others, or seized by overwhelming health issues that would impair judgment, attempting certain types of meditation, may not be advised, as it may cause these feelings to intensify. You are encouraged to consult with a licensed therapist or medical professional.

Sacred Space

As you declare sacred space for your meditation practice, there are things that you will need to keep organized and accessible.

Meditation Tools and Accessories:

- A prayer rug, yoga mat, and/or meditation cushion or stool can be all we need to symbolically declare the boundaries of our sacred space. A sacred circle of Light will form around us as we humble ourselves in praise, remembrance, and total submission to the Divine Will;

- Head covering to symbolize the closure of the Crown Chakra to all but the Energies of The Divine Oneness;

- Prayer beads to keep count in the repetition of mantras, prayers, and affirmations;

- A table with drawers, that is above waist level (standing), to place and store sacred, consecrated tools you will use for your practice;

- A white candle, ranging in size from a birthday cake candle to a seven-day candle. The flame of the candle represents the element of FIRE, the Original Flame of the One Divine Creator. White represents the Radiant Light of the Infinite Divine Essence. Do not light candles with matches because of the conflicting alchemical properties of Sulfur. Do not extinguish candles with your breath, so as not to scatter the energy of your intention. Use a candle snuffer;

- Incense holder, incense, and sage to represent the element of AIR. There are many types of incense with varied alchemical properties that attract and clear specific energies. Frankincense, myrrh, lavender, rose, and sage are only a few that resonate with the intention of your meditation. Though it is good to have knowledge of their properties and correspondences, I assert that the exercise of the soul's spiritual muscle and the energy of faithful prayer work is more important than what type of incense we are burning;

- Crystals, salt, a piece of organic fruit, or a plant representing the EARTH element and positive manifestation;

- A specific glass for water (used only for your meditation practice). It represents the element of WATER and its powerful, creative life-force. Speak the intention of your meditation into the glass of water. Use half to water the plant, and drink the other half;

- A journal, a calendar, and a specific ink pen (used only for your meditation practice).

Care for Tools and Accessories:

Meditation tools and accessories can absorb both positive and negative energies. They need to be cleansed periodically, whether they are stored or worn. There are many ways to cleanse accessories:

Recommended care for the sacred tools of a meditation practice varies from tradition to tradition. Basic protocol recommends keeping your accessories in a locked wooden box. It is not a good idea to let others, not even people that you consider close to you, handle your accessories when you are not present, *especially children.* Children are very sensitive and may play with them innocently, compromising their energy field. Wrapping them in silk or wool, and keeping them in a clean environment can protect the energy, vibration, and frequency of our accessories from the attachment of lower energies, entities, and vibrations. Pouches or scarves made of these materials can be found in any metaphysical book and supply store, or even better, we can add our personal touch, be creative, and make them ourselves. These accessories are easy to make and will provide the opportunity to stitch our own spiritual energy into every seam of the fabric.

The sun rising in the East signifies rebirth of the Timeless wisdom traditions. We face the East in our spiritual practices in full recognition and respect for what is known as the source of the wisdom of the ancients and the cradle of civilization. It is recommended to allow the items we use in our spiritual work to rest between sessions in the East, in a consecrated space that is clean, dark, and inaccessible to others.

Loaning, borrowing, or sharing spiritual tools is strongly discouraged.

Purchasing second-hand (used) spiritual accessories is not wise.

It is unwise to wear or carry items you consider sacred into environments that may compromise their energetic integrity.

We must never forget that none of the paraphernalia that decorates our sacred place defines or qualifies the nature of our spiritual work. Nor is it required for the success of our work. Our faith in the power of the Author of Mystic Law and all of creation holds the only power in our Healing Temple. The Temple of our spiritual dwelling is where *we* say it is. Our Sacred Tabernacle is in our head and in our heart. We are the gatekeepers of this mysterious portal of our soul's dwelling.

Out of respect, it is unwise to take spiritual accessories, symbols, or sacred literature, into unclean places such as the bathroom.

It is recommended that no sacred literature be stored or left in place below waist level, so keep that in mind when considering the height of the table you choose.

Sacred art is best reserved for display in designated places that are consecrated, clean, and free of nonresonant energies. Certain wall hangings with sacred inscriptions, though presented in the form of art, are never to be exposed to, or displayed in environments where lewd or disrespectful acts may be committed.

Avoid placing graven images on our altars, in our homes, cars, or the workplace, to keep our attention securely focused on the Unseen Realms of our spiritual work.

Care for Crystals:

Crystals can clear, transform, purify and balance stagnant, negative energy when worn, carried, or placed near the body. They interact with, and regenerate the vital centers of our subtle/energetic body. To protect yourselves and the items you hold sacred from the effects of absorbing negative energy, you must employ the basic practices of physical and spiritual cleanliness. Our sacred personal belongings have a distinguishing personality, a heartbeat, literally throbbing with energy. The more bonded we are to our spiritual accessories, the sooner we realize that they have a discernible pulse! They may appear inanimate, but they have life and energy. We must respect that. Crystals are a beautiful and powerful meditation tool. They are conductors of intense, healing energy, but you must be prepared to care for them in a very specific, prescribed manner, or their energy can turn destructive.

Our meditation accessories have an aura of their own. Their aura, much like our human aura, can attract and collect both positive and negative energy. Clear quartz crystals can help keep the electromagnetic field surrounding the physical body, as well as our accessories, clean and strong. Keeping a positive and clean aura is important. The aura reflects the condition of our spiritual, mental, emotional, and physical bodies. Our energy field appears as visible light and color to some who possess the gift of seeing auras. This magnetic force-field can become polluted and toxic, ultimately causing spiritual, mental, emotional, and physical illness.

The easiest way to perform a cleansing is to expose them to sunlight for a day or so. Soaking them in saltwater cleanses and recharges them. If there is no ocean access, they can be soaked overnight in a glass bowl of water containing one tablespoon of sea salt. Placing them on an amethyst crystal bed overnight also performs an energetic clearing or cleansing.

By respecting and preserving the energetic integrity of the tools we use in our spiritual practice, we are not "worshipping" the tools. We are respecting them for the service they provide us, and we are respecting ourselves as traveling the paths of wise, humble, and spiritually adept people.

The most basic knowledge of mystical practice informs us of the implications of exposing crystals, meditation beads, or any other sacred paraphernalia into toxic environments, such as bars or social settings where alcohol or drugs may be present. Some things go without saying. If we are wise enough to pursue such an advanced path of spirituality, we must be wise enough to understand how to protect ourselves and our spiritual tools and accessories, respecting their sacredness as well as our own.

The following affirmation is designed to assist in charging, dedicating, and activating crystals, candles, and other spiritual accessories. It is wise to be aware of explicit ritual protocol.

I am one with The Creator
From Spirit, I have come
To Spirit, I connect
We become as One

In the name of all
that is good and right

In the Name of Love
and Pure Divine Light

Join The "I in I" now
Join The "I in I" here
Dispel the shadows
Dispel the fear

Within this circle
of Light I cast
I heal the Karma
of lifetimes past

I banish the darkness
with this candle's flame
I offer this petition
in The Creator's Holy Name
For the highest good
of all concerned
With intention and Divine Will
this candle burns

According to Free Will
and harming none
So, must it be …
Divine Will be done

The Light Meditation

THE LIGHT MEDITATION

I AM PROTECTED AS THE ETERNAL LIGHT

Basic Guidelines to Follow for The Light Meditation

The Light Meditation should be performed before engaging in any spiritual ritual work or meditation. It is designed to cleanse and activate the energies of our Chakra System to facilitate balance, harmony, and protection. It is a useful meditation that can be practiced daily with your prayer of choice for energy maintenance and as a spiritual shield. This guided audio meditation is available as a download on the *dreamuniversalmedia.com* website. (See the Chapter called Meditation Download Instructions at the back of this book.) The transcript of the Light Meditation is presented here for your perusal to assure that you are aware of and aligned with all aspects of its content.

The Light Meditation
Transcript

I am seated in a comfortable position

facing the direction of the rising Sun

My back is straight

My feet are touching the floor

My hands rest palms up

I close my eyes

My mind's eye envisions

a single white candle that I light

with the intention of inner illumination

from my most profound depths

extending to the Origin of my existence

the Focal Point of Ultimate Light

From this comfortable seated position … I breathe

I am the observer … the witness of my breath

as it touches the middle of my upper lip

I observe the sensations for qualities

such as heat, coolness, moisture, dryness

I observe … undistracted by these sensations

I go within.

I slip between the invisible pockets of silence

between my inhaled and exhaled breath

My attention goes to the sensation of my breath

as it flows across the center groove of my upper lip

The focus of my awareness moves to my Solar Plexus

the 3rd Chakra

At its most profound point, there is an ethereal silver cord

anchored in my physical reality

to ground me … to guide me

back to the starting point of my journey if I should need it

A pinpoint of Light pulsates

to the rhythm of my heartbeat

and radiates from that focal point of Light

expanding to extend to, and beyond my entire body

enveloping me in this pure, radiant, protective Light

extending beyond me to envelop this room

extending beyond this room to envelop this entire building

this entire city and far beyond

seeking and connecting

to its Point of Origin.

I inhale through my nostrils

I exhale through my mouth

I inhale Light

I exhale fear

I cup my hands over my mouth

to collect sacred breath laced with golden Light and positive intention

I inhale Light and become it

I exhale fear and rebuke it

The silver cord that extends

from my navel area at the core of my being

dispels all fear as my consciousness drifts

It will guide me back

to my comfort zone

and starting point
whenever I choose

I cup my hands over my mouth
to collect the breath of my earnest petition
right hand over the left
good over evil
knowing one defines the other

My breath transmits
words of power
and utterances of commandments
a release
a surrender
of all that is of Maya's illusions
of all that is temporary
I release my attachment to the changeful
I embrace only the Unchanging
including the so-called "self"
of my own lower perceptions
I embrace all that I really am …
Breath, Awareness, Consciousness
the stillness that I AM

I suspend my senses
I shut down
I open up
Calm and focused breath
occurs in natural rhythms
I inhale through my nostrils
I exhale through my mouth

I inhale Light and become it
I exhale fear and rebuke it

I inhale golden Light
I cup my hands over my mouth
to collect my breath
laced with this golden Light and focused intention
I use it to dispel and cleanse unwelcome energies
It is charged with the intention of attracting the healing that I desire

With this sacred Light Breath
I wash my hands
then my face
of all carnal witnessing and unsavory desires
I cleanse my nose of the scent of the shadow worlds
my eyes … of all they have seen of suffering

I cleanse my Third-Eye … 6th Chakra
located between my eyebrows
of all it has observed of lower vibrations
My ears … of the filth they have heard

I cleanse my inner and outer voice at the throat level,
the energy vortex of my 5th Chakra
I cleanse thought-forms, both spoken and silenced, that traveled
on wings of words that injure like bullets and blades
I heal that with this sacred breath of radiant golden Light
I cleanse my Crown, 7th Chakra at the top of my head
of all that has ever sought to come between my Higher Self and my Source
the Source of all … The Ultimate Reality

With this sacred Light Breath

I move my attention down to the back of my neck

I cleanse and seal this entry point of whispered suggestions

from the lower planes of consciousness

seeking a home … seeking manifestation

through my mind and spirit

I cleanse my feet of every step they strayed

from the path of my enlightenment

with golden Light

of sacred breath

My footsteps are guided

My path is protected

My journey is blessed

I inhale Light and become it

I exhale fear and rebuke it

Hands cupped over my mouth,

right hand over the left,

I collect this sacred breath in my hands

I hold it to my heart

Healing cleansing energy of golden Light

enters my heart at my 4th Chakra

whirling, spinning, yielding in surrender

to my connection to Divinity

I accept that I am healed by this Breath of Light

I cleanse myself of the pain I have suffered that seeks to break me

I cleanse myself of emotional attachments to joy

that seeks to addict me and control me

I am not my emotions

I am not my past

I am not my future
I am not my mind
I am more than that

I break through the mirror of illusion
I forsake the lies that seek to define me
as less than an Eternal being of Divine Essence

I inhale through my nostrils
I exhale through my mouth
I inhale Light and become it
I exhale fear and rebuke it

I inhale Light
I cup my hands over my mouth to collect
breath laced with golden Light and positive intention

My mantra is
Thank You
My mantra is
Thank You

With this golden breath, I shield my Solar Plexus
from all energies that may seek to enter uninvited, unwelcome,
with their urges and weaknesses, cravings and clinging,
anger and unforgiveness, seeking to eclipse my will
with its self-serving obsessions and uncontrollable
desires and projections, seeking to make me believe they are my own

Sacred breath is the bridge between the many selves that I am
from the lower to the upper realms of consciousness

With it, I have cleansed and sealed this space that I am

I do not stand alone as its gatekeeper

I am protected from creation

That Which created me sustains me

I inhale through my nostrils

exhale through my mouth

I inhale Light and become it

I exhale fear and rebuke it

I inhale Light

I cup my hands over my mouth to collect

breath laced with golden Light and positive intention

With this breath, I shield my 2nd Chakra

located in the area of my lower abdomen

the seat of all desire, attachment, and aversion

With this sacred breath of pure golden Light

I suspend my senses

I cleanse the lower energetic, sensual,

carnal aspects of my being and heal them in the Eternal Now

The cleansing breath of golden Light subdues the raging fire of my Root Chakra

the 1st Chakra - Sacral Chakra

sending this creative energy rising into the golden Light

of the manifestation of my authority over my own animalistic nature

This primal fuel energizes all of the other chakras as it gently rises,

Uncoiled golden Light of purification

Rising

Up,

Up,

Up through the 2nd Chakra below the navel

Cleansing … Releasing negative energies

Up,

Up,

Up the Spine through the spiraling vortex of the 3rd Chakra

Spinning beautiful waves of golden Light

gently rushing up this life-enabling thread of creation's energy

Releasing … Cleansing … Healing … Illuminating

with golden waves of Light energy

sweeping clean all residue ... all debris

all attachments … all aversions … all longing for all else

but The Beloved … The Divine One

My mantra is

Thank You

My mantra is

Thank You

Cleansing Light gently rises through the 4TH Chakra … my heart …

healing it from the senseless acts of emotional savagery it has suffered …

Loving it for all of the Love it is capable of … trusting it with my life.

I close my body down

I am not my body

I am not my mind

I am not my emotions

I am more than that

I suspend my senses

I break the mirror of illusion

I meditate on the Light that I AM
the Light of the Eternal I AM

I have manifested on this plane
from the realm of the Divine One
I have expressed myself as my desire
for this Sacred Journey
from the angelic realm
the realm of the guides,
the realm of the Sacred
the abode of the prophets,
the mystics, the messengers, and servants
of the Most High GOD
Breath and Light are One
The Light of my Core Being
is One with the Core Point of Light
expressed out of triple darkness,
the Consciousness, the Love of the Ultimate I AM,
the Unknowable One, the Limitless One,
Whose name is best expressed by Silence.

My most sacred mantra is
Thank You

Beautiful energy has gathered in my Heart Chakra …
the Temple of my Beloved
the Temple of the Divine One
In Love … golden Light energy continues to rise … powerfully … subtly
Up through my 5th Chakra at my throat
Up through my 6th Chakra, my Third-Eye
Reaching the 7th Crown Chakra

Golden energy collected at the top of my head
connects with my strongest prayer

I pray

I pray for protection from all unwelcome,
uninvited energies
(silence during prayer)

Shhhhhhhhh
I accept this cloak of protection
enveloping the entire form of my body
physical and formless
cleansing my aura, purifying my intentions,
closing out all that is not of this protective Light
A pinpoint of Light pulsates to the rhythm of my heartbeat
and radiates from that focal point of Light
expanding to extend to and beyond my entire body
enveloping me in pure, radiant Light
extending beyond me to envelop this room
extending beyond this room to envelop this entire building
this entire city and far beyond … seeking and connecting
with all beings at the Point of Origin … pure consciousness
I breathe from my core
from the most profound center of my being
I cleanse myself with Sacred Breath
Golden Breath has become a solid shield of protection

Waves of beautiful golden Light
sweep up and over and around me

all the way up and over and around me

swirling up and over and around me

The Light is my Shield

It is my Comforter

I have always been That Light

My mantra is

Thank You

My mantra is

Thank You

I return from the silence … the stillness

grounded in my humble, energetic abode

anchored in the Safety I have affirmed

the Protection I have affirmed

the Love I have affirmed

the Freedom I have affirmed

I am released from guilt … released from shame …

released from judgment

If I have ventured out far enough to have trouble returning

I follow the silver cord extended from my navel

back to the state of consciousness that is awake and alert

aware, fully focused, and grounded

no longer corrupted by false identity and conditioning

The energy of this freedom washes over me in shimmering waves of assurance that

I am a being of Eternal Light … connected to all of creation

essentially connected to the Creator of all and I AFFIRM …

That which created me is sufficient to protect me!

I AM ONE WITH THAT!

****

The Light Meditation is available as an audio download at *dreamuniversalmedia.com*. Please see the instructions in the chapter "Meditation Download Instructions" at the back of this book. The Light Meditation is also available on our YouTube site: dreamuniversalmedia@youtube.com.

This section is an excerpt from my book FACELESS: THE SACRED RELATIONSHIP, a mystical journey behind the masks of the archetypal faces of the energies that permeate our lives. It is shared here as an in-depth overview and character analysis of a phenomenal energy that defies introduction or description. I share this, not as an archetype, or a personality. But as the Refuge in Whom we trust our souls. In such an overview of the influences "spirits" of varied descriptions can have on our lives … The Holy Spirit is the Ultimate, Most Powerful, and Relevant force and influence on the subject of the Dark Night of the Soul.

The Interceding Holy Spirit

Planetary Association – Preceded planets
Ruled by the Fifth Element – Light Akasha
Soul Star Chakra

As an archetype, in this text, the term Interceding Spirit (Holy Spirit) is not used in a "religious" context. It refers to a mystery that can only be called The Nameless, from a metaphysical perspective. A person who is in no way religious is just as available to the experience of this mysterious phenomenon as a person who rests firmly in the belief in The God and the spiritual hierarchy of their religion of choice. A nontheistic or atheistic person can just as easily become caught up in the throes of experiencing an array of diverse manifestations triggered by the power of the Holy Spirit. Regardless of their belief or non-belief system, one can appear to be triggered to exhibit apparently involuntary expressions, many no longer being in sovereign control of their 'person.'

Many religions, cultures, mystical paths, and belief systems seek to "own" exclusive rights to the access of the Holy Spirit, calling it by many names. Attempts at "ownership" are sometimes done through subtle, subconscious, subliminal references that are a part of our societal and spiritual conditioning. It is accomplished through media, tradition, culture, subliminal seduction, hegemony, thought-form implants, ethereal/energetic projections, and other control mechanisms, designed to manipulate mass consciousness. It is done through the whispered language of subconscious programming, boxes, and containers of identity, labels worn like toe tags, the viral hallucination of ownership of something that is NOT ownable. Perhaps these divisive manipulations are what has caused sayings like "the opiate of the masses" to be used in reference to these collective thought-form bubbles. These interpretations seek to establish, from the perspective of their own specific brand of hypnosis, that they, each in their own special way, are the "chosen ones." So many are waiting for a Chariot of some sort to swing low, scoop them up, and sweep them away, leaving behind everyone else who believe, think, and live their lives differently. That is all an element of the hypnosis. *However*, just behind this elaborately crafted veil of illusion, there is another version of "the collective" … The "Inclusive Collective," who, each in their own special way, *know* that we are *all* the chosen ones … each in our own special way.

If the Holy Spirit can *only* be experienced in a religious context, how do you explain phenomenal interventions in the lives of atheists or so-called non-believers, completely without solicitation, and unsupported by any particular belief system? Some, after having had "the experience," transcended religious references to explain what had happened to them. Many have categorized it as "Unknowable." There are marked, undeniable similarities among the reports of those who have succumbed to it or interacted with it. Bottom line, the experience of these interventions *transcend* religion, culture, race, ethnicity, personality, form, gender, Space and Time. It can only be classified as a *miracle* of the Unknowable Realm.

This Unconceivable Energetic Force is an element of The Absolute, The Ultimate, the Incomprehensible. A Force such as that cannot be an *object.* Some want to know or reason, "Is it male? Is it female? Is it neither, or is it both?" It is considered by many traditions or systems of belief to be beyond gender and human characteristics. Its Essence is insulted by being degraded to references of personhood that seek to reduce its presence to body parts, human features, and physical characteristics. It is inappropriate to attempt to assign it human appearances based on our own conditioning and finite understanding, even though it has been reported to have taken on a human appearance for its own time and purposes.

The Holy Spirit is not a person. It is a Spirit, but it is NOT a common spirit, as in references to jinn, ghosts, poltergeists, hauntings, or even angelic or elemental presences. It is The Inbreathing of Oneness with the Light and Essence of The Creator and the Out Breath of that Sacred Connection.

Across every mystical path and tradition (mostly in a religious context), characteristics of the Holy Spirit are consistently referred to, and described in many ways:

- It is a non-physical presence;
- It is made of Light or Self-illuminating triple darkness of dark matter/energy;
- It has no fixed form;
- It exists beyond Time and Space;
- It is memetic in nature, capable of shapeshifting apparitions;
- This Spirit can be experienced as Yin, Feminine and Receptive or Yang, Masculine and Interpenetrating and has no fixed gender;
- The Hebrew language *Ruach ha-Kodesh*, as well as the Arabic translation *Ruh al-Qudus (Ruach)* and *(Ruh),* are *feminine* references; and speak of the Divine aspect of prophecy and wisdom. Writers in these languages, commonly use maternal images when speaking of the Holy Spirit;
- The Christian Trinity manifests as The Father, Son, and Holy Spirit, commonly depicted as a winged dove, and as tongues of fire, holding that these are three aspects among the many manifestations of the One God;
- In the Catholic Church, the Holy Spirit is often referred to in English as "He," yet maintained that the established gender reference of each respective language should be upheld. Masculine gender references are common, yet understood to be *figurative* in reference to the personifications used when speaking of aspects

and attributes of The God, being that The God is Spirit and spirit has no fixed gender;

- Some paths of Christian belief teach that the Holy Spirit is of a feminine energy. Both feminine nouns and verbs, as well as feminine analogies, are thought to be used by The Bible to describe the Spirit of God;
- It is a manifestation of the Spirit of the Christ;
- It is a manifestation of the Spirit of the Mother of the Christ;
- It is often described as a Feminine energy;
- It is a manifestation of the Divine Feminine;
- The Bahai faith refers to it as the *"Most Great Spirit,"* the bounty of God;
- It is the vital, or animating force in all living things and creatures;
- It has an "in-dwelling" quality;
- In many literal translations, it is the *Breath of the God*;
- It is an aspect of Divine Grace;
- It has a viral quality, as though one may *transmit it* or *catch it*;
- It is capable of triggering or activating a spiritual awakening;
- It is an interpenetrating or occupying force, as in being *filled with it or full of it*;
- It is a conductive force, as one being made to *channel it*;
- It is a sentient force, as one being *touched by it*;
- It is a conduit in a manner that suggests transmission of diverse energies;
- It could cause one to be affected by it in some discernible way;
- It is completely beyond our linear understanding and expectations;
- It is completely beyond our concepts of Cause and Effect.

Elemental Qualities of the Interceding Spirit:

- *Fire Element:* It can be electrical in nature. There is an electrical current which associates its manifestations with the fire element, strong enough to literally knock a human down to the ground by invisible contact. Therefore, the Holy Spirit is understood to manifest as a destructive, fiery force in the context of a

150

cleansing, purging, sanctification, purification, or as an act of judgment. It can also refer to the fiery energy called Kundalini, surging up through the spinal column, from the 1st through the 7th Chakra. It is associated with fire as an element, in reference to being baptized by it, impassioned by it, or given it as a refined force in the context of prophecy and healing.

- *Water Element:* There are common references on many spiritual and mystical paths to being "baptized in the Holy Spirit" and being immersed or submerged in it. In this reference, the Holy Spirit and the water element are used synonymously. To be plunged beneath the water, and surface reborn symbolizes a strong force and source of great power to create change on an essential level. It also refers to bathing, washing, cleansing, and initiation of a process of purification. Associations with the water element extend to references of being "filled with it" as one would speak of filling an empty vessel with water, signifying replenishment or renewal. The references, "Water is a "type" of the Spirit of God," and "Water of Life," represent the Holy Spirit. In a reference, "I will pour out my Spirit," the water element speaks of the Holy Spirit.

- *Air Element:* The Holy Spirit is directly associated with breath, a breeze, a gust, burst, or torrent of wind. It can occur as having no apparent cause or source, a Force or phenomenon that 'touches' or makes a form of contact, creating a spontaneous effect. A forceful breath expelled from the mouth carrying sacred words, for the purpose of anointing, blessing, charging, or cleansing is also a manifestation of it. It also means *Life* as in *Breath of Life.* It is a manifestation of *air in motion,* like a *strong driving wind.* Air, like spirit, is invisible, but it can be perceived by normal senses. It can be heard. It can be felt. It can be seen through the manifestations of its effects. Breath when referencing communications can take on many forms. Spirit can communicate or speak through diverse mediums. Messages, revelations, even prophecy, can be transmitted through something that someone says at a particular moment, whether they are communicating directly to you, or not. These uncanny communications can travel by means of the airwaves, such as over the internet, television, radio, or through telepathic transmission directly to the mind.

- *Earth Element:* Most are familiar with the fact that demons have been known to operate in a form of what we identify as a "possession," with the ability to "take over" every aspect of a person's being. They may have the ability to speak, see, and hear through them, using their faculties. They are known to be able to impose or implant thoughts upon the mind, and command actions, without the knowledge or ability of the host to control what is happening. Outside of an extremely religious context, people don't talk as much about the energetic antithesis of such a phenomenon … The Holy Ghost/Spirit. In accounts that would be labeled miraculous, it has also been described of the Holy Spirit to be able to "take over" and compel a person who has been "touched" by it, or "filled" with it, to perform incredible manifestations of extraordinary or supernatural power. It has been described as an unknowable dynamistic Force that can appear either as personal or impersonal, and fill a person in a way similar to a fluid, permeating their entire presence.

- *Ether Element*: The Holy Spirit is associated with spiritual and mystical manifestations, a Presence in all major religions, and has been known to create manifestations in the lives of people who are atheists or completely indifferent to anything mystical in context. These events can occur by means of miraculous, spontaneous remissions in physical ailments, some of which may have been terminal, through a touch or energetic directive into the "human energy field" or aura.

It is believed to be able to travel in the auric field, in direct contact with the physical body, in such a way as to sustain it, protect it, and connect it with "higher" energies and forces. This Holy Ether or Akasha, occupying the Heart Chakra, is the full experience of the Omnipresent, Imperishable, and Unknowable, Ultimate Creative Force of all Being. From Ether, the revealer of all forms and names, all emerged. We do not have to be able to understand it or name it. Its existence is inarguable.

The Zeal Point Chakra - located in the back of the head at the base of the skull (the medulla oblongata) between the 2nd and 3rd cervical vertebrae. It is referred to as the "Mouth of God" and has a direct correlation to the energies of the Holy Spirit. The High-frequency conscious mind that masters expression of spiritual power through the voice.

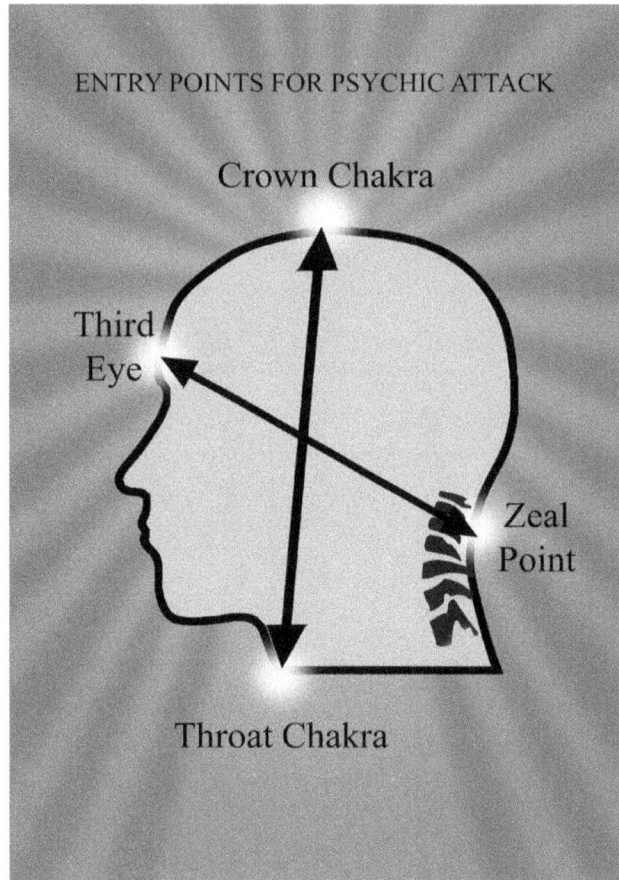

ENTRY POINTS FOR PSYCHIC ATTACK

Crown Chakra

Third
Eye

Zeal
Point

Throat Chakra

The Soul Star Chakra – the first of the Transpersonal Chakras (The Seat of the Soul), located just above ***The Crown Chakra***, the gateway of the energy flow into the body. Point of surrender to Divinity, the Holy Spirit, as our inner and guiding Light; where Transcendent Love and Spirit connect and are channeled into the physical body; Oneness with Divinity; selflessness and compassion; more ethereal, a higher octave of the function of the Crown Chakra, and is less available to egoic energies. The Soul Star Chakra connects us directly to the Cosmos, Ultimate Source, and the Holy Spirit.

The Fifth (Throat) Chakra is located in the throat region. 'Vishuddha' (meaning purification) is the Sanskrit word for the Fifth Chakra. It empowers us to mystically speak or channel Transcendent Truth. It is the crossroad point where the higher consciousness and physical body intersect. This energy vortex, where matter and spirit traverse, is associated with the Holy Spirit, revelation, inspiration, and communication. It is a portal through which high vibrational energies are drawn into both the subtle and physical bodies ... the gateway to Divine Light'. The Holy Spirit descends from the realms of pure, formless consciousness occurring as an indiscernible vibration that few can hear, capable of creating form.

When one has had an encounter with this Spirit, diverse manifestations include but are not limited to:

- Ecstatic states of consciousness with reports of feeling dissolved, absorbed by it, disappearing into it, merging with it, being filled with it, becoming one with it;

- Out of Body Experiences (OBE), a feeling of being taken away, out of the body, and returned to the body;

- Doubling over in a "crunch," consistent with being punched in the stomach;

- Quaking, the appearance of a seizure with no physical cause;

- Crying, weeping, laughing uncontrollably for no apparent reason;

- Behaving and appearing inebriated, staggering, communicating as though in a state of drunkenness. Loss of composure, muted or slurred speech, vacant or dizzied look in the eyes;

- Most report being indelibly "marked" in ways that people who know them consider remarkable. They note changes on every level of their being ... some common, some profound in nature;

- Describing the feeling as "good" by comparison to altered states of consciousness induced by alcohol or drugs;

- Complete loss of consciousness, fainting, falling out as though struck down by some unseen force. This phenomenon is called being "slain in the Spirit";

- Speaking or singing in tongues (unknown languages), a state called "glossolalia." Incoherent or prophetic outbursts for no apparent reason;

- Full body chills, goosebumps, tingling (feelings of effervescence), shivering, stiffening of the body;
- Spontaneous frenetic dancing, spinning, rapid whirling, giggling, hopping or jumping, rolling, running, unusual dancing;
- Prophetic visions and utterances, with or without mental images or words;
- The feeling of having been shown in words and imagery a "story," accompanied by the feeling of 'living in it, or often from an observer's perspective;
- Reacting like touching an electrical wire or cable. A fragile human frame being touched by that kind of energy is like a full-body shock.

MANIFESTATIONS include, but are not limited to:

- Distinct changes in the experiencer's character:
  o Their behavior;
  o Their disposition or attitude;
  o Their temperament;
  o Their sense of detachment from worldly affairs and concerns;
  o A shift of their striving or ambitions;
  o Their choice in associations;
  o The way they dress;
  o Their choices in music and entertainment;
  o Their choices in reading and studies;
  o The way they spend their money;
  o Their eating habits;
  o Their manner in handling personal relationships;
  o Their relationships with their children and other family members;
  o Their empathic concern for the poor and suffering;
  o Their preoccupation with ways of ending the suffering of others;
  o Their opposition to the oppression of self and others;
  o Their habits, drinking, smoking, drugs, and sexual behavior;

- o Their business practices;
- o The way they treat others;
- o The way they require themselves to be treated;
- o Their indifferent reaction to their own personal suffering or joy;
- o Unusual abilities to see into the spirit world;
- o Unusual abilities to interpret dreams;
- o Unusual abilities to create or compose (channel) art, music, poetry, and prose;
- o Intercessory prayer (on behalf of others).

- Charismatic gifts:
  - o Words of wisdom;
  - o Words of knowledge;
  - o Increased faith;
  - o The gift of healing;
  - o The gift of miracles;
  - o Prophecy;
  - o Discernment of spirits;
  - o Speaking in tongues;
  - o Interpretation of tongues.

These evidential manifestations cannot be reduced to the laws we recite of common cause and effect. The "Cause" is invisible to humans, yet visible "Effects" are witnessed. Rarely do you hear reports of people taking 'personal' credit for the incredible manifestation of the Holy Spirit. I am sure that a fear of being cut off would accompany any egoic claims of being the personal source of such power. The source of these gifts typically defy reason and are consistently attributed to the realm of Spirit.

- Grace:
  - o will fight for you;

- will intervene in your personal affairs;
- will grow your faith;
- will grow your understanding;
- will touch you;
- will comfort you;
- will heal you, and heal others through you.

The Spirit of Intercession is the manifest belief that the Holy Spirit is the ethereal guide, the Spirit of Absolute Grace, the Gift that intervenes in our affairs, in our state of love and surrender … or not. There are many who are far from being pious that report having been visited or touched by this mysterious Spirit, who have done absolutely nothing, by our judgment, to qualify. Some experiencers report that with the "electrical current" or "spark" of this touch, a state of "dissolving," suspension of the senses, a spontaneous spiritual awakening occurs. This often occurs after having fallen into hopelessness and helplessness to change the circumstances of their life. A mark is indelibly carved into the heart of one who has surrendered his or her personal will by the touch of the Holy Spirit.

The reason I refer to the archetype of the Holy Spirit as the "Interceding Spirit" is because I, as we all do, understand that in this life … Things go wrong. We can be made to feel powerless in the face of the whole ground being snatched from under our feet, finding ourselves left to deal with vulgar and uncouth opponents, apparently alone with no hope. Things go wrong in ways that appear they are not survivable. Yet, there are accounts of miracles that have occurred that defy explanation. There are testimonials and witnesses of a power, a force, beyond religious context, dogma, or understanding, that has miraculously intervened in the affairs of people's lives, often in a very personal way. Leaving a specific signature behind, there was a declaration of order established, a balance, and fairness restored. It is done by drawing from and being a conduit of the transmission of an Energy from the Highest Realms of Ultimate Transcendence, and *beyond* that, into the Absolutely Unknowable. It is believed to be the "Active" Force, Essential Spirit of The God, demonstrably projecting, as an Energy, through, to, and into anyone, any place, and at any time, just by Willing it, according to Divine Will. True accounts have defied reasonable explanation. For those who disbelieve, no proof is possible. For the latter, only direct experience could carry even a grain of proof.

The Holy Spirit is sometimes experienced as a Feminine or Yin energy. As her attribute, the manifestation of the Divine Feminine, she, in all of her creative, nurturing energy, is experiencing an incredible betrayal of her spirit. In the wake of her usurped power, she now attends an ill-conceived perpetual ceremony of the crowning of the "King." She stands in the ruins of her peaceful rulership, replaced by toxic masculine principles, imagery, and energies. Her tears flow in rivers. She sighs in resignation. In the face of the audacity of it all, she stands as the principle of the primordial womb. That is what perplexes the self-exalting, egoic traditional masculine principles, in denial of the nature of the non-dual True Self. In sacred scriptures, there are consistent references to Divinity as "We" in the context of gender. How could it be any other way?

God is used too often as a reference to an authoritative male Deity (with basic human characteristics and body parts) that dwells outside of one's self … that controls, surveils, rewards, and punishes, and requires a fear-based, rather than a love-based relationship. How could such a Force to be reckoned with be named and painted with the graffiti of personhood? How can any claim ownership of that which cannot be owned … only experienced?

If one's sad reality is completely anchored in contextual concepts of Cause and Effect, one will never understand the workings, the beauty of effects that occur with no 'apparent' cause. The gifts of the Holy Spirit are often given as a reward without evidently deserving it, a Grace, a Blessing … just because.

The Holy Spirit is beyond petition, beyond an altar, beyond prayer, beyond belief, beyond surrender, beyond perception … beyond the spiritual power structures of this plane of existence. The conspiracy of her complete disempowerment was accomplished by toxic masculine values that took control of industries that would influence and condition the world to disrespect her. And, for whatever reasons, even women fall under that spell and participate in their own spiritual dethroning. Within her womb, all creation found form, through her love it was born. At what point do the two opposite polarities of The Holy Spirit separate and become individuated hostile entities, operating in a conflicted sovereign way, no longer interdependent upon one another … each seeking to eclipse the Light of the other?

When the clouds of that shadow war descended, so did a collective forgetfulness … devouring the Light of beings that were trusted to be the portal, the womb into which the spirit is given to take form, issued onto this plane of experiencing. She was given to be the nest of its nurturing, the "channel," conduit, intermediary, the transitional vessel between the Realm of Divinity of the Spirit World in the realm of physical manifestation … whether she ever gives physical birth or not. She now rises up from the ashes of having been reduced to a caricature of a wicked imagination after having ultimately given up and reduced herself to that absurd level … if only in her own mind.

The "Divine Feminine" archetype is not a "person"ality steeped in "person"hood. This energy is not being presented as some "personal" concept of an in-dwelling or supportive entity. It is commonly believed in many spiritual and mystical traditions that there will be a "return" or a "revisiting" of the Holy Spirit to the "Mother Earth" to right wrongs and injustices experienced by the collective, bringing consequences and reckoning to the perpetrators of these inequities. The Nameless Secret, The Source of Transcendent Love, will heal and restore the wellbeing of this troubled world.

Whenever righteousness wanes
and unrighteousness increases,
I send myself forth.
For the protection of the good and for the destruction of evil,
and for the establishment of righteousness,
I come into being age after age.

~ Bhagavad Gita 4.7 –8 ~

References to the Holy Spirit are often used synonymously with The God, but not in a way as to establish associations with the Divine One. It is more acknowledged as a fusion of the Attributes of the One. The Unknowable One is beyond name, gender, translation, tongues, and utterances we use to describe it. For it to have a name, someone would have had to have been present at its birth to give it that name. How could that be? It is Birthless, Deathless, Faceless, Timeless, Limitless, Nameless, Selfless … Self-contained of every name, every attribute, and capable of every form, yet, beyond any mundane qualities, beyond all belief systems, philosophies, doctrines, or religions.

The compassionate voice of the Divine Feminine may petition, "Forgive them Holy Mother/Father, for they know not what they do." The energetic manifestations of Divine Feminine … These are our mothers, our companions, our daughters, our sisters, our teachers, our friends, our intermediary source. She symbolizes the Yin … dark matter, the dark energy of creation, from the plane of non-being, the self-illuminating triple darkness of the womb that birthed these beings into the manifest realm. The compassionate voice of the Divine Masculine may petition, "Forgive them Holy Mother/Father, for they know not what they do." The Ethereal manifestation of Divine Masculine … These are our fathers, our companions, our sons, our brothers, our teachers, our friends, our intermediary source. He symbolizes the Yang … emerging Light, the energy of creation, from the plane of non-being, the self-illuminating triple darkness of the womb that commanded these beings into the manifest realm.

We are not total opposites. We are not bags of body parts seeking to define the entirety of our being by physical attributes. We are energy, vibration, and frequency clothed in matter. Our existence occurs as two sides of the same coin … Indivisible. Each side contains the spirit of the other. But look closer. A coin does not have two sides, it has three sides. The third side is the energetic circumference that declares an interdependent oneness. We must meet on the third side, in the realm of the union of our peripheral reality as counterparts of the vehicle of existence, if we want to avert the dire consequences of gender-based wars. These bodies are our vehicles, not our weapons against one another. We are Light. We must accept ourselves as Light, energy, and pure consciousness on the third side. The paradox.

Engaging in a relationship with any aspect of The Holy Spirit archetype begins with the awareness of its sacred nature and its relevance in regard to the well-being of the planet and its beings. Generally, and with regard to relationships, this energy transcends identification as a mere "archetype." We must expand our perceptions and become one with the Spirit and allow it to guide and protect us, and fill us full of its Light. When hope is gone, when all is lost, the spirit of renewal rises up and shines out of the eyes of the formerly hopeless, who found Her voice in their heart.

A whisper arises from the threshold of the Realm of Turiya … "You are not alone. You cannot do this on your own. You were never *required* to do this on your own. You have no "own." You are my own, and I am your own. Grace exists as you. Be confirmed in that!" whispers the Deliverer and Origin of Grace.

I have been a seeker and I still am,
but I stopped asking the books and the stars.
I started listening to the teaching of my Soul.

~ Rumi~

The Holy Spirit is an Intervening Spirit of Truth and is partial, unlike impartial spirits, entities, and energies that might be called upon to defend or protect you, expecting favors or offerings in return, unbeknownst to you.

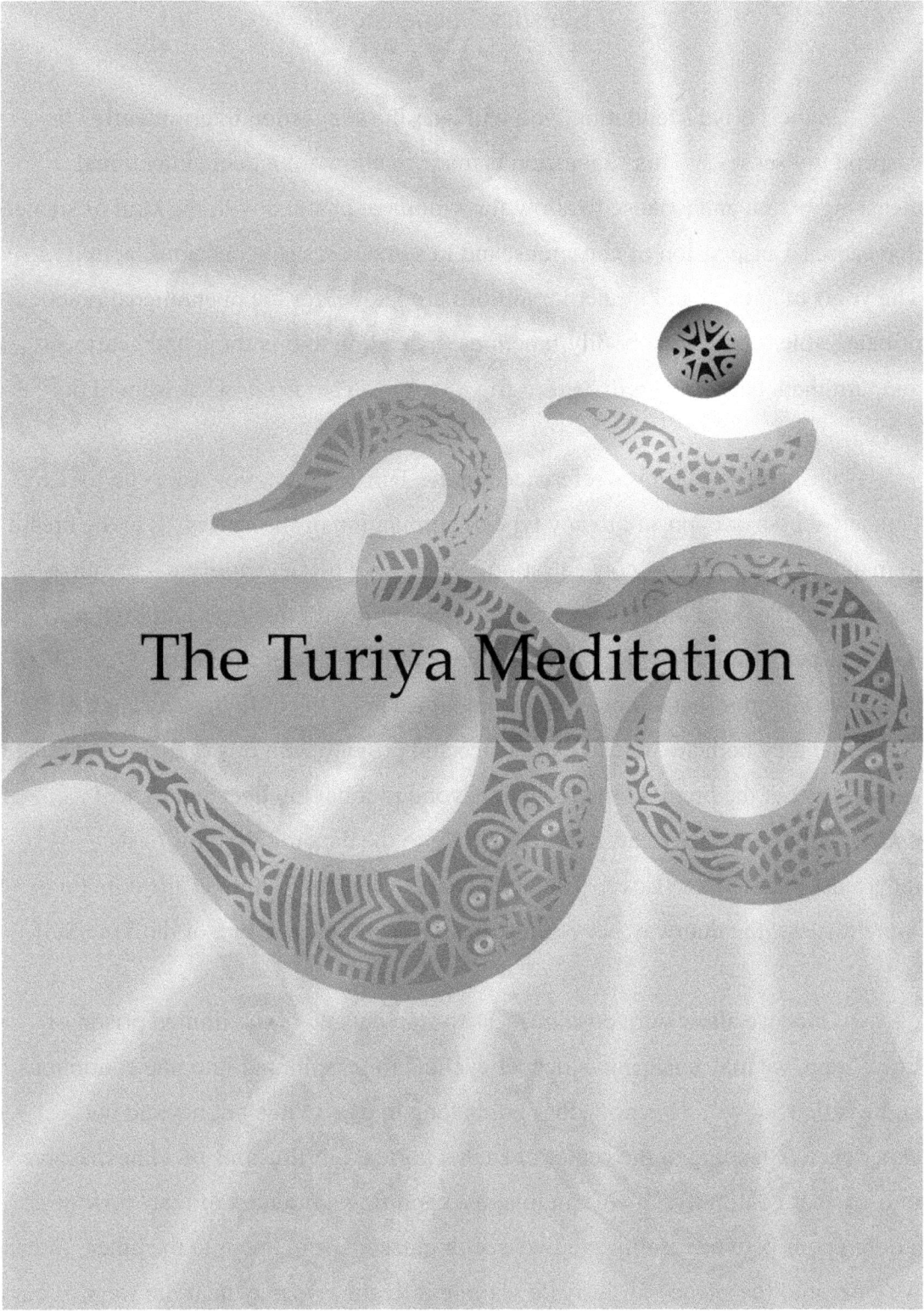

The Turiya Meditation

Sensory Suspension

In the Turiya Meditation, you will hear the suggestion intermittently, "I suspend my senses." This suggestion is made to allow for a deep, intentional cleansing breath and a pause to allow for a moment charged with the kind of silence that causes a suspension of conscious, and in some cases subconscious, activity. The yogis of ancient and modern traditions are known for the phenomenal practice of being able to stop vital bodily functions (extending to breathing and heartbeat) and turn them back on at will as if to flip a switch. That is *not* what we will do.

Suspension of senses referenced in the Turiya Meditation asks you to deny yourself access or exposure to any type of stimulation of the senses. Use the breath to maintain high levels of concentration. What we will do is hold each breath as sacred, still the mind into the silence by replacing it with the heart and rhythmic beat that sustains it, allowing the brain to rest in the place of the heart. We will let those two energies that are perceived sometimes to be in conflict, savoring the peace that they both are able to experience and provide with this dramatic yet gentle exchange. Let the brain do the feeling, beyond rational intellect and logical understanding. Let the heart do the thinking, to the dancing rhythms of its innermost transcendent Love. The heart beats to a silent rhythm of the domain of Timelessness, the doorway between realms. Remain in the State of the True Self.

Once we allow our consciousness to step outside of the limited prison of linear time, we may enter into a deeper cyclical time, spinning into one continuous circle called "now." This now does not belong to us, yet it is not beyond our experience. Standing in the center of such a vortex, our illusions of Time dissolve into circular continuity. If we can imagine capturing a moment of that "now-ness," a door opens between realms, and we see or enter … from one into the other. When we enter into the silence of Turiya's realmless Realm, we may hear the story of our souls told like a nursery rhyme of a Self we have never known. It has always been there, just behind all of our perceived versions of ourselves, as the witness or observer. Our True Self will silence all other stories, as the Truth of our being steps out to live our most authentic life.

We are sentient beings. Most of us are more reactive to outer sensual stimuli than what befits a higher quality experience of life. That leaves us at the mercy of energies, influences, and forces that often do not have our highest good as their agenda. We are often vulnerable to triggers we cannot even trace back to their actual source. The common senses will be asked to take momentary pauses as a brief surrender, throughout the meditation, just to take them off of overdrive.

We have five primary physical senses (hearing, sight, smell, taste, touch), each with a multitude of dimensions of expression. When we "suspend" the senses, our level of concentration has become so hyper-focused that we withdraw our attention from sounds, sights, smells, tastes, touch, or any related sensual thoughts of the past, present, or future. It is difficult to duplicate the kind of environment one would experience in an isolation/floatation tank.

Total sensory deprivation is virtually impossible unless you have been able to design a life around being able to make it possible. Generally, one must illicit control over non-physical 'space' in order to accomplish the level of silence required for deep-state meditation practice. Many rely on practices that help to control these normal human urges and cravings. The goal is not necessarily renunciation or abstinence, just modification, and control. We have the freedom to choose one state of consciousness over another. We can choose to suspend our senses, rather than being triggered by the experience of stimuli such as changes in temperature, sexual energy, hunger pangs, physical, mental, and emotional pain, or issues with a sense of balance and vibration. Once the body adjusts to the sensation of "nothingness," the stress centers of the brain relax and release less cortisol (the chemical connected to our stress levels). Lowering levels of sensory input has been demonstrated to improve a range of ailments and emotional states such as anxiety, trauma, depression, and chronic pain issues. It has been known to increase problem-solving, technical, and creative skills.

The experience of meditating in a floatation tank moves the consciousness from alpha and beta to the theta waves one experiences briefly just before falling asleep and waking up. Extended Theta States can trigger dramatic mental imagery and intense visions, even in the waking state. With the brain's relaxed response to the cessation of sensory input, it is common to experience vivid mental imagery and visualize strong images you wouldn't normally see, even extending to the experience of hallucinations. In more extreme cases, people have experienced Out-of-Body, Astral Projection, and Sleep Paralysis events, which require strong psychic shielding to consider safe.

In certain systems of meditation, it is possible to achieve and sustain this state, even *without* intending to. It can take years of practice to achieve Theta State at will, but it has also been known to happen spontaneously as a result of intense psychological, physical, or emotional triggers. That is why it is important to include practices of psychic protection in your meditation practice and be acquainted with some of the dangers of meditation as well as its benefits.

There are ways to intentionally interrupt or reduce sensory input using a light-blocking eye mask, earplugs or headphones, wearing loose cotton or linen clothing, avoiding scents (cologne, perfume, scented lotions, or creams), jewelry, hair ornaments, or styles that may create a distraction. It is such a challenge in today's fast-paced, densely structured world, to completely isolate ourselves from other people and manage not to be disturbed. Establish a practice of allowing time away from busy schedules and social environments to self-isolate and heal.

We transcend thoughts related to the senses by removing body/mind identification and Time/Space consciousness. We will transcend the mental chatter of mindless, mundane preoccupations, and singularly focus on any sense that is normally stimulated within the body until it falls under our control. Our senses provide the data for perception. Senses are enhanced through a committed practice of mystical/transcendental meditation.

We naturally possess what is known as "Extra Sensory Perception," "Sixth Sense," and a state spoken of as having a "Third-Eye" open. When part of your brain stops getting input in a state of being sensory deprived, other parts of the brain will seek to compensate, activating senses we are not consciously aware of. These states manifest as ethereal components of normal brain activity and may lead to phenomena known as:

- Clairvoyance;
- Clairaudience;
- Clairsentience;
- Transtemporal Experience – refers to how the passage of time is perceived and experienced; transcending time; related to time travel or to the influence of, or communication between one time and another;
- Access to transcendent realities, i.e., Prophetic Realm, healings from the Angelic Realm;
- Interference of, assistance from, or interaction with hyper-dimensional beings (Refer to my book FEARLESS; PSYCHIC SELF-DEFENSE for important information regarding protocol for handling such occurrences).

The HU Mantra

The intonement of "HU" is believed to be the True Nameless Name of The God, one that no path or traveler on it can claim ownership of. It is a mystical, vibratory expression of a oneness that is beyond language, beyond the comprehension of this mundane plane of names and forms. It refers to the Supreme Being beyond the Unknowable Plane of Zero-Point Negative Existence. From ancient times the wise ones have conjured many names from many languages, traditions, and cultures. In the wake of that noise was the Silence of the mystics, as it was in the beginning. But they knew, there was always Something there ... Some Unknowable Something ... Beyond the thought of form ... Beyond the imagination of Absolute Immeasurable Potential.

HU is the first manifestation of the Ultimate Breath ... the Vibration, the Frequency, the Ultimate Cause of everything, known and Unknown. HU is the Breath, the Voice, the Sacred innermost Spirit, and Song of all things. Creation dissolves all identity in the infinite ocean of stillness and harmonizes in the silent song of surrender to the "HU." All of creation exhales the last breath of longing, with the dreams and illusions of separation, annihilated and surrendered into the Oneness of "HU."

The HU mantra is the spiritual *Source* as well as the *Completion* of all sound, all words, all being. The keeper of the secret of sound guards the mystery of creation. Timeless revelation has spun Light and shadow worlds, in and out of healing the excruciating pangs of suffering, impermanence, attachment, and aversion. From obscurity to illumination, through the manifest and unmanifest, mortal, and Eternal ... through the HU, we find the healing of perishable creation in the realms of the infinite. Sound vibration charges and cleans all seven bodies and their energy points, activates the Solar Plexus, recharges the central nervous system, as it balances and aligns the chakras. This mantra is a life-sustaining tool for reducing anxiety, insomnia, fear, and depression, focusing on connecting the body and the soul with the Oneness of Hu.

- The HU is chanted similarly to the OM (AUM) as "Huuuuuuu. . .";
- HU is the emanation of the abstract plane, meaning unlimited sound;
- HU creates an absorption into the Oneness of Ultimate Reality;
- It symbolizes Union with The God;
- All sound is based on HU;
- HU is the Zikr of Silence;
- It harmonizes negative frequencies, chakras, energy points, and energetic bodies;
- The vibrations of HU are too subtle to be perceptible to the physical senses;
- HU activates the non-physical aspect of the sense of hearing;
- Heavenly Emanation of the Essential aspect of Breath;
- The sound of the Source of all sources;
- All sounds have their uniqueness until they all finally become Hu;
- HU is known as Abstract Sound, Primordial Sound, referring to its authorless nature;
- It collapses all distinctions, dualities, and constructs;
- It collapses all distinctions of concepts and precepts;
- It collapses the time barriers of past, present, and future;
- It collapses distinctions between physical inner space and outer space. It is in, it is out, it is around, and it is about;
- It is a door/portal/vortex of energy that dissolves the ego and increases inner Light;
- HU collapses all realms into the Unknowable;
- It allows the True Self to effortlessly transcend all planes of existence, freed from all the limitations of mundane reality;

- Transcendence through the HU mantra can approach and exceed states of rapture;

- One may enter a state of extreme intoxication, manifesting as symptoms such as trance state, i.e., fixed stare, dilated pupils, dreamy facial expression, blissful glow, expressions of an otherworldly quality;

- HU can inspire experiences of the unseen worlds in the form of receiving intuitions, visions, and revelations. Impressions of Divine wisdom may be imparted in experiences with the Holy Spirit;

- One may experience a release from pain, anxiety, worries, fear, and sorrow, as the soul feels freed from the imprisonment of the senses and the physical body;

- It kills fear, anger, sadness, depression, ego, hate, arrogance, envy, and jealousy;

- The HU mantra can keep others from controlling you;

- It is a powerful tool of Manifestation;

- Sound and vibration of HU is the Source of inner revelation;

- The mystics of all traditions know that sound vibration has a peculiar effect on every aspect of Universal existence;

- The mystery of HU is revealed to the Mystic;

- When the abstract sound is audible, all other sounds become indistinct to the mystic;

- Yogis and ascetics experience HU through Breath, as is experienced in song, the shankha conch shell, ney flute, reed flute, and didgeridoo. It leads to the awakening of the inner life and connection with the inner tone.

Turiya Meditation Transcript

I am seated in a comfortable position

facing the direction of the rising Sun.

My back is straight.

My feet are touching the floor.

My hands rest palms up

on my knees.

I close my eyes.

My mind's eye envisions

a single white candle

that I light with the intention

of inner illumination

from my most profound depths

extending to the Origin of my existence

the Focal Point of Ultimate Light

I INHALE

I EXHALE

My attention goes to the sensation of my breath

as it flows across the center groove on my upper lip

I INHALE

I EXHALE

The focus of my awareness moves to my Solar Plexus

At its most profound point, there is an ethereal Silver Cord

anchored in my physical reality

to ground me … to guide me back

to the starting point of my journey

if I should need it

A pinpoint of Light pulsates

to the rhythm of my heartbeat

and *radiates* from that focal point of Light

expanding to extend to, and beyond my entire body

enveloping me in pure, radiant, protective Light

reaching beyond me to envelop this entire room

extending beyond this room to envelop this entire building

this entire city ... and far beyond

seeking and connecting

full circle

to its Point of Origin.

From this comfortable seated position

I BREATHE

Who am I?

Why am I even here?

Where am I from ... really?

I AM beyond the veil between worlds

I AM beyond the threshold of Maya, The Illusory World

I AM in this world but I AM not of this world

I AM the Unknowable Fourth State

I AM TURIYA

I AM PURE CONSCIOUS AWARENESS

I suspend my senses

I go within.

I cannot be understood intellectually

I can only be understood by direct experience

I can communicate with you through direct transmission

I AM Timeless awareness

I express the nature of Absolute Reality

I AM beyond thought

I AM TURIYA

I AM PURE CONSCIOUS AWARENESS

I suspend my senses
I go within.

I AM beyond concept
I AM beyond floating as buoyant energy waves
I AM beyond pulsing in the rhythmic heartbeat of all creation
I AM beyond vibration
I AM beyond the misty, ethereal quality of dew on petals of a rose at dawn
I AM beyond the violet Light of the 7th energy center at the top of my head

I AM beyond the footprints my weary feet
have left behind me
in the sands of time
I AM TURIYA
I AM PURE CONSCIOUS AWARENESS

I suspend my senses
I go within.

I AM not attached to being right … or more
I AM before the word 'surrender'
Before there was anything to surrender to
I AM One with Creator and all of creation in this blissful surrender
I AM beyond having to explain what is happening to me, even to myself

I am before relaxation
at the deepest level of stillness
I am before sleep
beyond the deepest level of slumber
The True Self is free of all of these
I am before dreaming myself into wakefulness
I AM TURIYA
I AM PURE CONSCIOUS AWARENESS
I suspend my senses
I go within.

I am subtle worlds and dense matter
I AM a braided loop of waking mindfulness,
Ether, and deep sleep Dreamtime States

I am both latent unconsciousness
and the luminous transcendence
of my vast energy field

I AM the Realm of Mystic Union
beyond the Veil,
beyond desire, beyond the absence of desire,
beyond Zero-Point Negative Existence, egoless absence of identity
I AM TURIYA
I AM PURE CONSCIOUS AWARENESS

I suspend my senses
I go within.

I AM beyond the Observer perspective of Infinite Reality
There is nothing and no one left to observe
There is no "me" … The idea of "me" has disappeared
There is no "I" … The idea of "I" is absorbed back
into the elements from which it willfully arose
I AM beyond the being … weightless, spacious, passing clouds
blown across the sky of my witnessing
I AM beyond the destabilizing, shape-shifting,
fragile forms I have assumed
as I INHALE
sacred breaths of renunciations of illusion
I EXHALE
Past
I EXHALE
Future
I AM TURIYA
I AM PURE CONSCIOUS AWARENESS

I suspend my senses
I go within.

No story
No attachment
No aversion
No Time … No Space

No Cause … No Effect
No Memory
No Forgetfulness
I AM TURIYA
I AM PURE CONSCIOUS AWARENESS

I suspend my senses
I go within.

I AM
beyond birth
beyond body
beyond mind
beyond labels
beyond race
beyond gender
beyond agenda
beyond description
beyond language
I AM beyond
sensations of Timelessness
beyond dreaming
beyond peace
and mindfulness
I AM TURIYA
I AM PURE CONSCIOUS AWARENESS

I suspend my senses
I go within.

I awake as awareness surrenders
to Divine Nameless, Faceless Reality
Question it or rationalize it … and it disappears
This sweet surrender is an **IN**-the body-experience
There is no particular brand of conditioning
that this Unknowable Reality belongs to
It is not an event that can be hosted by anyone
It can only be accepted as Pure Grace
from a "Now" that does not belong to us

from the Breathless Breath of the Fourth Moment
I AM ONE WITH TURIYA
I AM PURE CONSCIOUS AWARENESS

I suspend my senses
I go within.

I am One with THAT, right here, right now,
in and out of Time and Space!

I am One with THAT!

HU

HU whispered into
my namelessness
HU are you ancient soul?
beyond breath
beyond death
HU are you ancient soul?
beyond merge
beyond purge
Do you know HU I AM?

Go within.

Otherness disappears into oneness
Within disappears into without
Torn from what I once called me
now a paralyzed wave
adrift on a shoreless sea
beyond the agony
beyond the ecstasy
beyond belief
beyond hypocrisy
beyond the "I"
beyond the "me"

HU are you ancient soul?
There is no distinction
between the Light within

and the Light without
There's no distinction
No shadows ... No doubt
There is no distinction
between faint whispers
and piercing screams
between piety
and blasphemy

HU are you ancient soul?
There is no distinction
between music and silence
Holy Water and tears
agony and ecstasy
courage and fear

HU are you ancient soul?
You are the limitless wave
I am the limitless sea
The ache of the longing
is the remembrance of me
Do you know who you are?
Do you know Who I AM?
For you to know
You must
go within.

I return from the silence

the stillness

renewed

grounded in my humble, energetic abode

anchored in the SAFETY I have affirmed

the PROTECTION I have affirmed

the LOVE I have affirmed

the FREEDOM I have affirmed

Released from guilt

Released from shame

Released from judgment

Released from blame

I give up all hope for a better past

If I have ventured out far enough to have trouble returning
I follow the silver cord extended from my navel
back to the state of consciousness that is awake and alert,
aware, fully focused, and grounded
no longer corrupted by false identity and conditioning

The energy of this freedom washes over me in shimmering waves of assurance
that I am a being of Eternal Light ... connected to all of creation
essentially connected to the Creator of all
and I AFFIRM
That which created me is sufficient to protect me!
I AFFIRM

I AM ONE WITH THAT!

The True Self

Meditation and Ego Death

Meditation can be a bridge between false perceptions of reality and Ultimate reality. My book, THE TIMELESS NOW: Healing from Grief and Loss, features the *I Transcend My Ego Self* meditation, a guided meditation that begins an exploratory voyage through the wisdom of the ancients and beyond the door of the fear of death. The journey begins with how we perceive ourselves on the other side of the Self-Inquiry that begins with the question, "Who am I?"

As I stepped into becoming the answer to that question, I AM … the revelation had begun. Self-Inquiry is the fixing of one's focus on the inner reality of Self, or "I," as pure awareness witnessing the body vehicle. It is the dismantling of conditioned structures that seek to define the self in one-dimensional and purely physical terms. To hold our attention on the witness as "I" offers the freeing opportunity to experience the formless, True, Timeless, Eternal Self.

Through Self-Inquiry and a study of the Universal Law of Impermanence, I sought the fluid state of Self-Realization, wherein we embrace the sacred transition from what we call "life," into an unknown territory of Life beyond life. Meditations of this and many other types can free the non-physical Self from the physical self, enough to produce the experience of an altered state of consciousness. An experience of being pure awareness or Nirvana can free one from the perpetually spinning Karmic wheel of life, death, and rebirth, if only during the Timeless moments of the meditation. It may be a state we find difficult to remain in, but at least it introduces us to an energy we can evoke and revisit at will. The Sanskrit word Nirvana refers to the extinction of all concepts and identity and the subsequent state of bliss. It is known by many different names from many different traditions; Satori, Kensho, Moksha, Paradise, Fanaa, Turiya, Sacchidananda, and Samadhi are only a few.

A taste of this ethereal state of consciousness can even occur spontaneously. I have experienced it. As terrifying as it was to me, when I realized I had looked deeply into the eyes of Impermanence, I was released into a state of Ego Death or being "slain in the spirit." I disappeared to myself as if I had fallen through a hole in Time. I died to my ego self. Awareness embraced both nothingness and expansiveness, releasing me from all concepts of suffering.

The *I Transcend My Ego Self* meditation allows us the perspective of the observer of our own sacred transition. We are able to realize that change can be a terrifying passage or a welcome reprieve. It depends on how we choose to experience the fact that we are not the body. Even when the body falls away, we are still there as something that does not change and cannot die. We meditatively transcend our attachment to the physical body vehicle at will, in total embrace of the essence, the consciousness that we really are. The Light body accepts the bittersweet shift of perception as the formless Self merges with the Ultimate reality. It patiently waits for the soul's return with loving, open arms, even for the brief visits in meditation and prayer.

Who am I?

"Who am I?" is a question of transcendence. Being that our most essential Self is Spirit, it is reasonable to experience the domain of The Holy Spirit, The Holy Ether of The Creator, through which we experience spiritual strength and resilience. We do not have to understand it or turn it into a religion to have a healing relationship with it. Through prayer and diligent meditation practice, we exercise the muscle of complete submission to The Will of The Divine. When we choose to live a surrendered life, we are rewarded with courage, sufficient to quell the sense of foreboding that will naturally wrench our egos at the thought of the world we have come to know without us in it. That thought sends shudders of paralyzing fear through to the core of the being of a mind conditioned by fear and attachment to identification with physical forms. We begin to understand that we were in the picture we see of this world before we were born into it, just not in our present form. So, the question is, "Where were we?" When our faces are erased from the canvas we call the mirror, where will we be then? But, particularly, are these "places" really so distant from one another? Are they "places" at all? We are the designers of temporal reality and seek to define a distinct past, present, and future. We have the power to engage a filter that refines our reality to the point of fluid redefinition, all variances merging into the all-encompassing now. Who we really are is Timeless, unchanging in this changeful world.

Let Go

Our goal is to meditatively let go of our attachment to the physical form and mundane realities that lead to a fear of death that is so overwhelming it disturbs our experience of life. As we perform this intense spiritual contemplation, we train our mind's eye to look into the mirror and not see the vehicle, and look into the eyes of Eternity to see our souls. The vehicle comes, and it goes. The driver, our soul, that Eternal, formless being who we really are, does not come and go. It does not die. We are energy, and energy cannot be created or destroyed. As our essence, we existed before we entered the body vehicle, and we will not cease to exist without it. With this profound insight, we can take responsibility for the health and well-being of our Essential Self as a Light body, and see the positive results of our efforts manifested in the quality of our lives. We seek to concern ourselves less with all of the persons, places, and things that come and go. We find that which does not come and go; that changeless space; the Eternal Being; who we really are, and focus on that.

Our Blessing

The Universe becomes our playground, but not our toy. This is not a game. I do not recommend a mere cursory study of the practice of Mystical Meditation. To ignore its complexity is to miss the benefits of its simplicity. Practice and commitment can evolve into an abundantly free spirit, able to navigate the whirlwinds of circumstance. The goal of this text is to encourage the acceptance of our responsibility as builders of our innermost sacred temple, that we may retreat there from the linear, superficial values that often serve as obstacles to our transcendence into the consciousness of the Eternal.

Beginning with this spiritual study and work, we are reaching into the archives of the mysteries of the ancients for tools that will help us on our path to peace of mind. These tools are used with spiritual authority and responsibility. They are tentacles used to plug into age-old systems that can allow the transmission of truth and guidance. We seek to manifest the Desire of the Divine Oneness upon the unique design of our destiny.

We seek to respect, love, nurture, and energetically sculpt our formless, imageless Light body, into the awareness of the perfection, the connection, the Eternal I AM that it already is. We accept that we are shape-shifting Lightworkers in this time of spiritual awakening. We are beings of conscious Light in Timeless Oneness with the Eternal Essence, whether we realize it or not.

At the crossroads of my spiritual journey, there were helpers. At every twist and turn along the way, there was guidance, seen and unseen. The highest aspiration is to be a pointing for others. The path reveals more than the destination. The path is the destination. The embrace of the Sacred Law of Impermanence allowed me to accept that pain is the flip side of the coin of joy. It evolves from a practice into a spontaneous way of being.

Self-Inquiry Meditation

A Course in Miracles teaches that "The self that needs protecting is not real." Most mystical paths teach, "We are not our bodies. We are not our thoughts. We are not our feelings. We are not our fears. The True Self is more than that." Between provocation and reaction to the triggering, there is a breath empty of ego. A single breath is an opportunity, a processor of thought and thought-form, a moment between being and "nothing." In that space is our power to choose our response. In our response lies our growth and our freedom."

For me, the transcendence of fear of hyper-dimensional interferences began with Vipassana, India's ancient meditation technique. Vipassana translates from Sanskrit to basically mean "insight" or "prajna," insight into the true nature of reality. It is as a veil lifted to allow seeing the essential nature of things as they really are, with lucidity and clarity of mind. The objective of the Vipassana meditation practice is to free oneself from the bondage of suffering by cultivating perspectives that transcend the body/mind attachment to responding emotionally to every sensation that would cause the experience of fear.

The most powerful perspective I have found is to know the True Self, remain "*as*" the True Self, and know that our animating personal breath is a Breath shared with us of the Divine One … and our connection to the Ultimate Self. The ultimate epiphany of consciousness comes in the knowledge that these beings cannot enter the Realm of Divinity, as we are able to. We follow that breath to its Source. There, is our refuge.

I do not know how to keep a secular perspective in this expression, and I do not promote or denounce the "religious" beliefs of anyone. The purpose of this text is not to tell anyone what to believe in. I only wish to share perspectives. I see the "True Self" as being the animating life-force, entrusted to us by the

Creator of this shell, that houses who we really are. I also see the word "God" (as Creator) being recklessly used as a divisive thought-form, even ascribed basic characteristics of common 'personhood,' having the potential for incredible suffering and destruction.

Within the context of our inherent Oneness with The Creator Being of our Highest understanding, we are absorbed into Timeless Light. Whatever THAT is … We are THAT, holding fast to the knowledge that we did not create ourselves … What created us has the Ultimate Power to protect, heal, and sustain us. Our True Essence is not of the nature of our physical being. That is why God "concepts" are consigned to the realm of the Unknowable on many sacred mystical paths because it is pure egoic vanity to claim to "know" the Unknowable.

I know nothing. I AM nothing. I *still* say that my prayers, and my sacrifices, my life, as well as my death, are all for, and belonging to the Realmless Realm of That Unknowable One, that I have experienced. The Breath that permeates and animates this reed flute is All that I AM. I *seek* Oneness. I AM Oneness. The illusion of separation subsides, dissolves into The All There Is, into the same Self-Illuminating Triple Darkness from which we emerged, in loving surrender.

The Dark Night of the Soul is a mystical process that can naturally lead us into realms of consciousness beyond the Physical Plane of existence. A high enough dose of stress, fear, and grief can catapult our body of consciousness into the lower Astral Realms, even if we don't know what the Astral realm is. The beings of that realm are more diverse than the beings of this one. We won't necessarily know what we are dealing with. In some cases, opportunistic, malefic beings of that plane may seek to take advantage of our vulnerable situation. Encounters with these beings, on the spectrum of experience, could range anywhere from mild curiosity or benign mischief, to potentially threatening, even dangerous events.

This is not to evoke fear. Since the beginnings of time, mystical remedies have worked to bring order to this type of chaos. A meditation that works for me as an effective deterrent for managing fears of lower Astral Realm drama and its sometimes harmful agendas is a practice called Self-Inquiry (Self-Enquiry). I was introduced to this meditation through the techniques of Non-Dual, Advaita, Zen philosophies, particularly those of Bhagavan Sri Ramana Maharshi, the Sage of Arunachala, an acclaimed, Indian guru/mystic (30 December 1879 – 14 April 1950). In the practice of Self-Inquiry, one focuses on "abiding as the Self" … the True Self … reaching the point of Ultimate Self-ness with one repetitive question, "WHO AM I?" No meditation practice I know of more directly addresses the phenomenon of a spontaneous Turiya event, triggered by a The Dark Night of the Soul experience than that one. The false projections and fake identities that sought to incorrectly define our being, fade with the awareness of the 'I AM not' … not this body … not this mind … not this fear … not alone. The meditation is complete when the meditator disappears … disappears to false branding and labeling … disappears to perspectives and desires of the lower self … disappears to everything that one is not. What is left? That is who we are. That is the answer … silence, consciousness, Light.

The word "ego" has many interpretations. It can refer to personal self-worth, self-confidence, or in a psychological context may refer to the mediator between the subconscious and conscious mind, a manifestation of "*person*ality" and individuated body/mind identification. We must become the knowing of the difference between "me" and "I," or we are nothing but a corpse on the pathway to a hole in the ground. When we ask ourselves, "Who am I?" we must know we can't find "I" in the mirror. The True Self, the "I," the "I in I," the I AM, nonphysical awareness/consciousness that is unique to our being, yet not unique to all things … That is who we truly are. When we find ourselves on the outside of the body vehicle looking at it, voluntarily or involuntarily, for whatever reason, we must know that the cold, inanimate shell is not who we are. When lifted by the liberating embrace of a Turiya experience, it is more important than ever to remember that … We are One with That Which manifested it.

In the process of a Turiya experience, when one may feel ejected from the physical body, self-perception is invaluable. We may look down upon that helpless body lying there, and know that it is not who we really are. Body/mind identification in the context of a mystical event is an obstacle. It is a product of the ever-busy ego, constructing and reconstructing, remodeling, repurposing, rewiring, redefining the Self as some AI-bot drone that is here to live, consume, and die, and just do what it is told. Obey! Then these conditioned priorities get placed on the back burner of a life-disrupting phenomenon that is beyond common understanding. Who we really are is *not* powerless or helpless. Self-Inquiry specifically triggers identification as the True Self, as the principal means to transcend the illusion of body/mind self-classification, and abide as pure Self-Awareness, surrendering to the experience of Oneness with the Unknowable.

At the age of 16, Sri Ramana Maharshi had a "death-experience" which paralleled the symptoms and manifestations of a classic Sleep Paralysis event, which also shares some qualities of a Turiya experience. The experience of that 'episode' left his body "rigid with the sudden fear of death," struck by what he called, "a flash of excitement" or "heat." He became aware of a "current" or "force" that seemed to "possess" him. He witnessed himself as the True "I" or "Self" and observed himself as having dissolved into Oneness with the Supreme Being. His devotees communicate that he ultimately realized that "the body dies, but that the "current" or "force" remains alive." The observer, or witness, inquiring within, *"What sees the seer?"* … saw the seer disappear, leaving only That which stands forever." This is the foundation of the Self-Inquiry meditation that extends beyond releasing the fear of the shadows that life naturally casts, to the release of the fear of death itself. One asks in meditation and contemplation, as did Sri Ramana, "What is it that dies and what is Eternal?" … then, the "current" or "force" is identified as the Realized Self, the True Self.

The introspective question "Who am I?" does not use any specific object as a focal point, rather it observes transcendence of body/mind identifications into Zero-Point Negative Existence. Again, this question is not asked to "answer the question." It is asked to dissolve the questioner.

- The Self-Inquiry method is an interrogation that makes the mind enter into a state of void.
- Repetition of the Yogic/Vedantic negation, "Neti, Neti. (Not this, nor that)" begins to peel back the layers of labels and conditioning that blind us to who we really are. "I am not this body. I am not this mind. I am not this reflection in the mirror. I am not this story I am telling myself of who I am. I am not …"
- We become the witness to the emergence of the True Self (with no concepts, no conditioning, no attributes, no story, no mind, no form, no past, no future, no time, no attachments, no aversions).
- We become transpersonal consciousness, aware of the pure awareness beyond duality, beyond intellect, beyond agenda, beyond memory, beyond gender, beyond linear thinking, beyond rationale, neither this nor that … the Unknowable.
- The Ultimate Self cannot be known by our mundane manners of thinking. With that acceptance, a kind of *surrender* presents itself to a once loud, busy, distracted, delusional mind and brings a True Self-centered peace of mind and contentment.
- The elimination of all that was believed to be known allows space for revelation, rising up from the silence.
- Only by eliminating what is known (our thoughts, perceptions, and emotions) is it possible to reveal to the linear mind the Ultimate "I," the I in I, the Eternal Now.

- We immerse and dissolve ourselves into the knowingness that becomes increasingly visceral and profound in this revelation of our own True Nature, who we really are.

- The question itself is born from *stillness,* and it is also fed from the *silence* that is home to our mind and our inner being.

- The question rises up from the spaciousness to name the nameless, to define the undefinable, as just That … undefinable.

- As our realization of the True Self reveals our Oneness with/as Divine Existence … We disappear to oppression, becoming unavailable as a victim to any oppressor who cannot enter into the Realm of Divinity, our True Origin and place of our refuge.

- What appears to be a void, is seen as Self-illuminating Triple Darkness, latent Light, the spontaneous, immeasurable awareness of who we really are. The question "Who am I?" exists within us in a dormant state and emanates manifestation of the harmony of our entire complex being. This harmony ignites the flame of Self-Realization and recognition of our Union and relationship with Divine Existence.

- Upon what feels like the 'death bed' of the questioner, the question arises, "Who am I?" The answer frees the sufferer of false identity. The True Self observes and answers, "I AM!" The spell, the hypnosis of false-identifications is broken.

Keep the "I am"
at the focal point of awareness
in the focus of awareness,
Remember that "you are,"
Watch yourself ceaselessly.
Give up all questions
Except one: "Who am I?"
After all, the only fact
that you are sure of
is that "you are."
The "I am" is certain.

The "I am this" is not.
Struggle to find out
What you are in reality
Relax and watch the "I am."
Reality is just behind it.
Keep quiet, keep silent;
It will emerge.
or rather,
it will take you in

~ Sri Nisargadatta Maharaj~

The Inquiry MUST prevail … Who is the body that "I" am hovering above? How is it that all that would animate it to life is still with "me," floating here in some bizarre, nonphysical state of being? My thoughts are with "me." My emotions, what I would call the "soul" of my being … It is all with "me," the "I" that observes the inanimate body encased in the names, words, labels, evaluations, and judgments, that made it feel "real." So, who is that body, the one I've seen in all of my mirrors, in transitional phases of its existence? Who am I? The beginning of Self-Inquiry. Who am I? Which one is my True Self? Identification only as the physical "self" is the most dangerous of the deceptions of Maya, the illusory realm of existence. In Maya, the nonphysical is visible as it vibrates at a lower rate of speed. It is slowed down enough to trick a Timeless, imperishable, formless being into believing that its defining reality is only what can be seen with ordinary vision.

The Meaning of the I AM

The I AM defies definition. We are dreams born of the sacred realm of the I AM, delicately clothed in matter. Only the blind spots of our own vision would make us believe otherwise. There are many common names for the energy of this subtle and powerful field of conscious energy. There are many manifestations of the I AM. It is the object of our Self-Inquiry, that conversation between the ego self and the Higher Self. The energy of the formless, Eternal, transcendent being of pure consciousness is the Higher Self that we are. The I AM has deep significance in many mystical traditions and goes back into antiquity thousands of years, representing a pure, Timeless, formless Self that witnesses the physical expression of Itself as us. We manifest in form as the clay creatures we are, driven by That Sacred Breath, powered by That Light of Origin, sustained by the same. The heart must embrace this perspective to be released from the bondage of self-identification with transient forms covered with labels and become a truly Self-Realized being. This is not an event. It is a path through the mystical gates of Self-awareness, into the Eternal domain of the I AM that we are.

The I AM seems to represent something different to everyone. Historically, the I AM has no definition since its presence precedes those who might seek to define it. It has come to represent a cry for home, for freedom from captivity, a cry for The God. As a key element of regular spiritual practice, many metaphorically burn or "chant down" all of the false identities assumed in our efforts to assimilate into this theatre of shadows. The simple act of ignoring false precepts and concepts of Self facilitates the burning away of counterfeit inner and outer realities that lead us to our spiritual corruption and destruction.

The vibration associated with the I AM can be maintained through disciplined spiritual practice, faith, and reliance on the seen and unseen for guidance. It is represented in this text as a dimension of consciousness accessible to all of us, for WE are the temple that houses the energies of the Eternal I AM, the Creator of all we are and all we know. It is only a matter of exercising and flexing the muscle of remaining in the I AM, pulling ourselves back from every cage of bogus definition we assign to our True Self. Even though notions of Eternal existence are commonly associated with a past life, a future life, or an afterlife, it can be entered without experiencing what we call death. To view existence as the I AM or to remain within the myopic vision of a one-dimensional self-concept is a choice. When we have suffered sufficiently from this limiting and terrifying perspective, we expand our focus to explore the nature of who we really are.

Who we really are is not limited to that reflection we see in the mirror. Even the mirror has enough sense to know that our reflection is not who we are, so it does not cling to anything we show it. It accepts and releases. It does not look for yesterday or tomorrow. It does not record or identify with that image. It is our own minds that tend to do that. But we are not the mind. We are not the body. We are That … That which preceded the mirror and all false concepts of the "I." The real "I" is that formless, Timeless, storyless being expressing itself as the form it witnesses in the mirror. "That" is the I AM. From that perspective, we ask, "Who am I?" From this perspective, we affirm that there is no death, no time, no story, no form. Then, after the rush of freedom we feel from that realization, we must ask, "Can the seer be seen? Can the witness be witnessed? What witnesses the witness?" At this point, Self-Inquiry begins. The fire is kindled, and the process of awakening to freedom has begun. Time is escaped. The bullying of the flesh is checked and put in its place as a cooperative subordinate to the Higher Self and the Most High.

From a state of consciousness mimicking a coma, we awaken to the dawn of every new day, rejoicing that we are blessed with the opportunity to renew our commitment to the purification of our hearts. We commit ourselves to cleansing the controlling, manipulative energies of desire, attachment, and aversion. There are many roads to the spiritual mindset of the I AM. There are many names ascribed to the Ultimate Witness. Opinions, cultural conditioning, and choices only add to the diversity of the colorful mosaic of our collective journey. The fact that someone else is traveling a different path than our own does not mean that they are lost. There should be no unfavorable comparisons, nor should these paths and respective deities be set up in competition with one another for rightness. If we have images, qualities, or even the intonation of a name, that reference is still not of the Ultimate I AM, the Unknowable, and most subtle in density.

In the Baha'i temple in Wilmette, Illinois, one of the most beautiful I have ever seen, there are nine doors, each representing a different faith. Each of the doors represents a path to the experience of what is characterized in this text as the Realm of the I AM, the Realm of the Sacred. There is nothing that must be done to earn one's place as the I AM, only to strive to gracefully master the balance of unconditional acceptance of the perfect balance inherent in creation. Everything has a balance that must be kept to progress from negative into positive existence. There is no such thing as all good or all bad. That type of terminology is subjective, relative, and can turn on a dime. Communicating this philosophy is the sacred symbol commonly referred to as the Yin Yang.

The Yin Yang is a sacred symbol that represents all of life as a circle, rather than seeing it as linear. A horizontal timeline suggests that there is a distinct beginning and an ending. A vertical timeline may suggest the same. But there is no end within the circle, especially this circle. It is divided into two parts, not in a straight line, but an "S" shape. One side is black, illustrating the Void from which the Light emerged. The white side illustrates the Light. The two small circles of opposite polarity on each side mean that nothing is just one way. Duality is our nature and the nature of creation. It requires us to be more merciful and compassionate in our judgments of everything, including ourselves. Everything and everyone is a composite of two sides, each necessary to the other.

Whatever name you want to call it, and there are many, our souls are well familiar with the energies of I AM, naturally seeking its serenity for survival. The longing is the connection. If prayer were a government, its name would be I AM. Its flag and national anthem would be "the Eternal OM." Its race is the *human* race. The President's name could only be expressed by silence. The I AM is our safe refuge from the evil influences and attacks of mischievous creation. The streets on this sacred journey are littered with broken hearts and vanity-based dreams. That Which Created us is sufficient to guide us through the challenging experience of material form and will be there waiting to welcome our grateful spirits home. Unconditional Love is the Soul of the I AM.

The Ego Under Attack

That ego "I" image of us is so full of vanity-based energy, spinning in such powerfully distracting circles of illusion, that it often cannot defend itself from the attacks of psychic bullies. That is the first thing any bully attacks, the ego of the intended victim. This malevolent spirit stalks, looking for weaknesses, tentatively sensing someplace for the attack to land, some open door of the psyche through which to direct the negative energy. As it is on the playgrounds of the schoolyards of the world, so it is in the cosmos, on the physical and ethereal planes. That type of energy predates our collective history on this planet. However, if there is no fertile soil to root in, no hump to ride, there is nowhere for that plane to land. It's got to keep on flying, generally on the flight plan of a boomerang. Journaling will show you how the surrendering of the false "I," ego-based identities, naturally coincides with the dismantling of psychic attacks and attackers.

If we feel some aspect of our life is under attack, we must ask the "I," Self, "WHO is the target of this attack?" Who is the "I" that experiences the phenomena associated with this attack? Is it the "I," me, my, mine, one-dimensional self-concept? Or is it the formless, nameless, identity-less "I" of the Eternal I AM that expresses itself as us ... the shadowy forms we take far too seriously, and at the same time, not seriously enough. Who is that "I" that is under attack?

The stereotypical attacker is generally targeting the "I" we see in the mirror. What defends the "I" is the "I" that can only be seen with the eye of the soul, The I AM. It is secure in its defense because the Ultimate "I" witnesses all and can and will intervene in our affairs. The psychology of the attacker is petty and shallow in its mental perceptions and projections. It is covetous. It is jealous. It is mean. It is cruel. It has a hunger that can only be satiated by the suffering of others. It preys upon the vulnerable at their weakest point and strikes below the belt to the heart of ego self identity. It literally chants down its victim until those voices become a shared mantra. The victim then joins the attacker in the dismantling of his or her self-esteem. Often the target becomes depressed and takes on self-destructive behaviors … all symptoms, rather than the cause. Rarely is the attack without motive, as senseless as it may be. More often than not, the attack is rooted in some form of competitive jealousy, or some level of malignant envy. The attacker perceives the intended victim as having something that they feel was denied to them, and that they are worthier of it. They may become overwhelmed by uncontrollable, self-serving compulsions that they feel are best satisfied by violating others, passively, aggressively or both. Generally, these far-reaching tentacles extend out of empty desire, fueled by narcissistic ego self identity.

The attacker who wages war against the innocent does not approach from a position of strength, security, or confidence. They are blind to the knowledge of their own Higher Self and choose to operate from the shadow realm due to thought-forms of "not enough." Happy, secure people don't act that way. This sort of an attack can even be unintentional, a wicked thought-form riding on the wind of a full Moon, damaged pride, hatred, and low self-esteem.

Attackers count on a runway into our consciousness, welcoming any and everything that tries to land there. If we do not provide a landing strip, if we do not allow our own egos to leave our psychic doors open, many attacking energies will escape our awareness. To ignore the ocean, and respond to every wave of emotion and judgment, is to become the attacker of our own peace of mind and well-being. As an attacker of self, we are then robbed of our primary advantage as a spiritual warrior, our innocence.

An attack of any sort is a gamble riskier than feeling drunk and lucky in a Vegas casino on payday. When someone initiates an attack, they have no way of knowing what they are up against. After scrutinizing a person believed to be known, even intimately, by the attacker, there is *still* no possible way to truly predict how the target will respond to being attacked. It is not possible to know the victim.

Upon determining that it is the ego self "I" that is under attack, it is important to process raw emotions of anger and counter aggression, seeking a refined form of energetic expression. For example, imagine we find ourselves in a situation where someone is sending desperate, attacking energy, targeting us based on a perception that it is we who are triggering those feelings within him or her. That doubles their anger. First, they are disturbed by what they know or see that sparks their envy, jealousy, or hatred. Then enters the distorted perception that it is the fault of the perceived trigger of their energy, and that person is to blame for *their* suffering. There is never an acknowledgment of personal responsibility.

"Hater" is a word that started as slang but has found its way into mainstream vernacular. Everyone knows what a "hater" is, and we all have a few in our lives, no matter what we do. All we can do about it is not become one. All we can do about it is keep our energy grounded in spiritual integrity and gratitude for the blessings we have and our faith in The God. There is an army of forces, energies, and entities already set in place that is sufficient to protect and guide our Souls under Universal Law. We are not even required or advised to petition to them directly. All we are required to do is surrender to Divine Will and respect the ongoing process of that sacred surrender.

A study, practice, and discipline of meditation will allow us to see life from a witness or observer's perspective, even a Timeless perspective, from which we are better able to understand Time and the relationship between it and the events of our lives. We also view our journey from a Time-circle that we stand in the center of, rather than a "timeline." We are in uncharted territory. Meditation is a valuable tool for connecting the dots of the messages, signs, and visions we receive. The words "random" and "coincidence" have no place in our consciousness. Every aspect of our existence is Intentional.

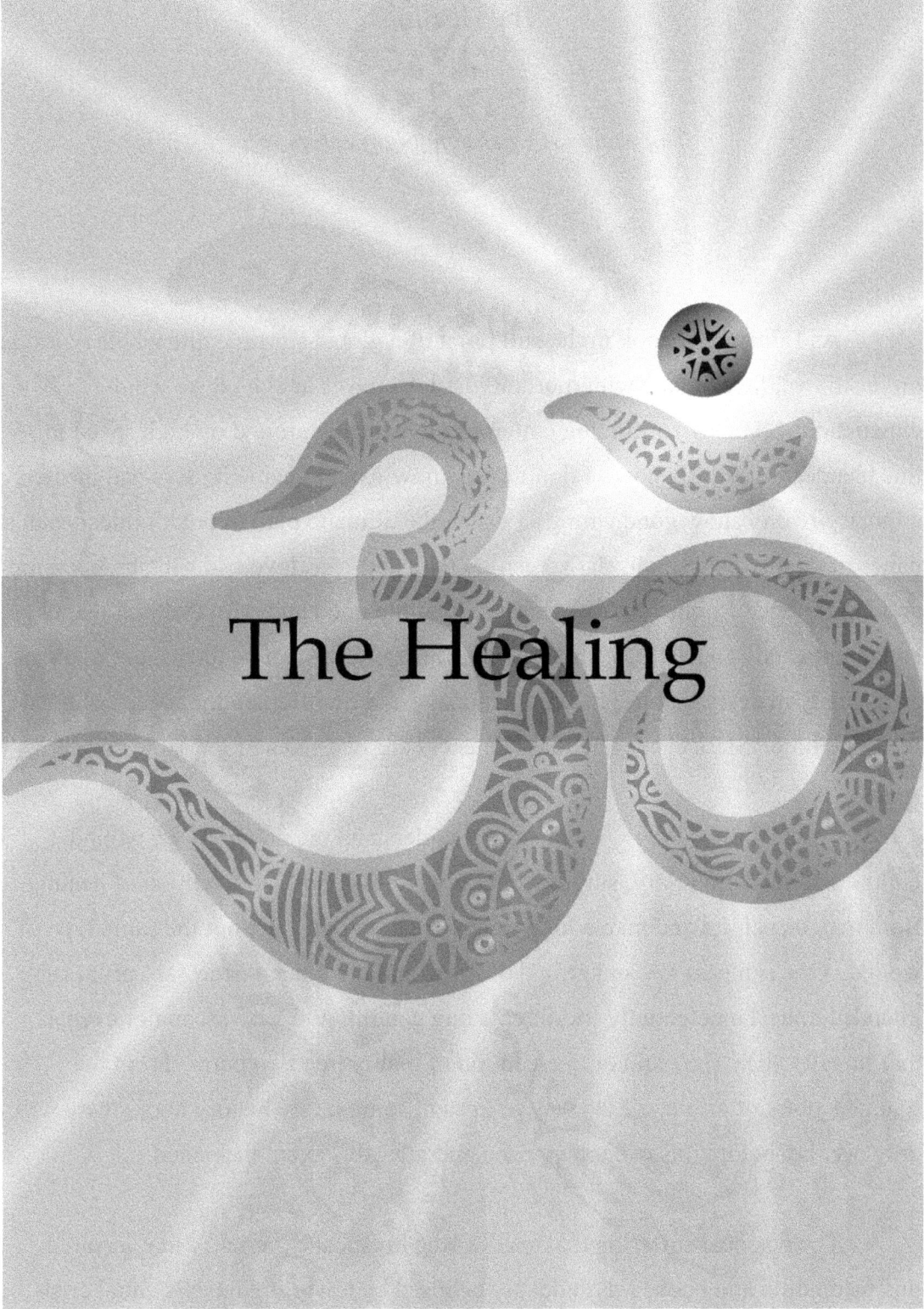

The Healing

The Healing

The wound is where the Light enters you.

~ Rumi ~

As I finish this book in the still point of a global storm … the whole world is on lockdown, face to face with mortality issues I never imagined we would experience. So many conflicting emotions are whirling around on high speed in this blender we call life now. I don't even know what to name it. It is bad theater, a fantasy/reality show gone wrong. I watch the ultimate play of polar opposites in a dance of duality on a small, flat-screen … faith and fear, love and hate, compassion and indifference … one might even say incredible good and pure evil, malignant egophrenia and ego death. The mass trauma in its wake can be the trigger to a mass awakening, in every culture, in every language and tradition on the planet … all at the same time. Mass chaos and mass Oneness are two sides of the same coin.

For healing to begin, we must first understand the nature of the wound. Unlike a street-fight injury, surgery creates wounding with an intention of healing. Both may be painful and take a long time to heal, but they are not the same type of wound. One is meant to damage and destroy, and the other a necessary procedure intended to heal a potentially life-threatening condition. There are major events that literally slice Time and our perception of reality into two parts. From the trauma's point of origin, all the way to lines in some future history book, there will only ever be, before this event happened and after this event happened.

The personal suffering that sparked the mystical experience that inspired this meditation and book, was suddenly eclipsed by a worldwide existential crisis. It is now of such overwhelming proportions that any egoic self-interest I entertained prior to this became a river of vain expectations, flooding into a sea of false hope, fading from my memory. I recall having felt alone and abandoned by the illusions I once held about life, along with everything and everyone in it. I felt like a boat without a sail adrift in a sea of the sorrow of having never mattered. In retrospect, it was boot-camp training, only a warning shot for what was to come.

Falling asleep in one world and waking up in another, never to be the same again, is as much a concept beyond my reach, as it is to the rest of the world. Now here we all are, between the sword and the wall, trauma-bonded for having shared in this horrific, Dark Night of the Soul experience. The question is, what do we do about it? How do we heal ourselves from this death blow? It is too soon to consider beginning a healing journey. It is not and may never be over. Because of the level of shattering of the former self, it may be awkward to enter into Self-Inquiry meditation, asking, 'Who Am I?' We must begin by asking, "Who am I **NOW**? As a collective, we may make this inquiry inclusive and ask, "Who are We **NOW**?" Allow these questions to initiate a profound Self-Inquiry meditation.

I believe in the mystery, the Magick, and the power of naming things. The energy, frequency, and vibration of language has the capacity to, not only alter what we may have believed to be fixed realities, but also alter our cells and evolve our conditioned patterns of thought and behavior, as long as it is aligned with Divine Will. Naming things gives us the authority to use language to either empower or diminish the quality of our lives.

As we find ourselves among the ashes of fallen realities, we must rise like the proverbial phoenix and seek to **IDENTIFY** a new reality, and **NAME** it. To name something is to *evoke* it and issue it into being, just like magick. Further, to **UNDERSTAND** it is a form of **EXORCISM**. Identify the invading thought-form construct as fear, a debilitating, hopeless, existential fear. **UNDERSTAND** that the creator of all things known and unknown is our source of strength, of Light, of Sustenance, and Deliverance. **REMEMBRANCE** of The *Law of Impermanence*, activated by spiritual practice, is the **EXORCISM** of the invading thought-form of **FEAR.**

Whether or not this can be healed, depends on how the question, " Who am I now," is answered. The correct answer is, "I am the same unchangeful, Eternal being that I was before this happened, even though Time drew a line that split itself in half … before this happened and after this happened. I am of the Realm of the Timeless." Then, "Who are we now as a collective?" The correct answer is "we are the same unchangeful, Eternal beings that we were before this happened, before Time drew a line that split itself in half … before this happened and after this happened. We are of the Realm of the Timeless."

When a person or a collective descends into a Dark Night of the Soul experience, someone had a hand in that process. There must have been a sense of ownership in place, leading them to a perception of entitlement to do as they pleased.

To find peace and healing, we must first **IDENTIFY**, **NAME**, and **UNDERSTAND** the old reality. I identify it and name it Bondage versus Freedom. The *understanding* of it is the exorcism of it, the breaking of the spell. What happens to the spell casters? They lose power by default over the newly identified reality because they did not name it. It is not theirs anymore. Name it *Freedom*. Name it *Good over evil, "every time."* Name it *Light*. Then, Live it *abundantly*.

We subconsciously cling to consensus realities and social constructs that yield false identities and acceptable images, based on … "Who do "I" want to be seen as by others?" The caricatures we draw of ourselves can be our worst enemies. Failing to drop these veils and masks can rob us of our authenticity to the extent that we do not recognize or love ourselves for one primary reason … we don't know the True Self of our individual or collective being. Whatever we

NAME it, let it begin with "TRUE" … beginning with the revelation of The "True" Self of our highest understanding.

I sought to study and NAME this mysterious state of consciousness that spontaneously visits following the experience of some traumatic event. In my case, it was a meditative state of consciousness called Turiya, which shared many characteristics of Samadhi. Both are generally achieved through a committed spiritual and meditation practice. Whatever plane of existence I had inadvertently landed on, or dissolved into, sparked a research frenzy that resulted in much of the information in this book. My intention was to share this refuge from the madness of lower realities that had somehow found me cocooned in a Koreatown ashram.

I'm not going to try to conform this sharing to some empty cliché, steeped in duality, called "positive vibes only." Positive and negative is a judgment, which is subjective. Everyone's "positive" is different. What is positive to the spider is negative to the fly. Are we awake? Are we paying attention? As it relates to personal ego death, it is generally traced back to a person or people acting as a provocateur, with an agenda to incite a certain reaction. In the case of "mass ego death," a shared "event" and experience manipulates and shifts realities to trigger a level of disorientation that distorts the identity of the experiencers. The shift of norms causes identity mutations that strip the ego's attachment to the former perceptions of self. Are we going to focus on the trigger, or are we going to focus on healing the damage done by the bullet lodged in our collective hearts? The bullet is the experience of this loss of our core sense of self that leaves us struggling to either find ourselves or reconstruct the shattered ego. What we need is a New Self that better accommodates the True Self.

The True Self does not experience the shattering because it is as unchanging as the Source in the shared Essence of Divinity. The ego is not necessarily "evil." It is what makes us human. What do we gain by hunting and killing it when it only needs to be healed? Seeking to kill it is just another ego activity and not an interest of the unthreatened True Self. Don't kill it. Observe it without judgment. Talk to it. Warn it. Tell it, "You are trying to be a shadow, but I will drag you into the Light." Initiate a self-activating, perpetual healing session with a secure shield and filter designed to disarm and neutralize attempted assaults against the True Self.

Being strong does not require our denial of the pain we feel. We just have to identify *who* is feeling it. Is it the fearful ego clinging desperately to an illusion that we created as an identity we have become the slave of? It is definitely not the True Self engaged in this battle. The True Self is the observer of it. When we get tired enough of senseless suffering, we will stand up and become the co-recreators of our reality in personal freedom and sovereignty in the Light of our Essential Self. The panic, even the fear, and hopelessness we are feeling, will be transmuted into the strength of Surrendering this, and every day, to Divine Will ... because that is all that can happen. We can shrink into duality or rise into trust and name it Love ... whether we understand it or not. It is beyond our realm of understanding, but not beyond the realm of our Knowing.

"It is time to sound our muted voices in the unseen realms, not to beg and bargain for favors of some *"other"* outside of the True Self, to restore a past that is gone, that hurt more than it ever healed. Raise as One harmonious voice, a song of gratitude for That Light within, the connection it has with its Source, and the miracle of Co-creation. Our indelible signature must be our offering to call out from the shadows of any Self-Illuminating Triple Darkness across Time, and command, "Let there be Light!" Realize our Oneness with it.

While the spotlight of Babylonian influenced cultures focuses on status, appearances, and negative comparisons, sacrificing an endless array of body parts upon the magical altar of the superficial, mundane and profane ... we are all the same on an Essential level. In the heated drama of violent competition, we cannot see our sameness because our differences are being programmed to divide us and make us miserable. When looking for differences, a healthy ego directs us to look within, and ask, "Who am I, really? How is the life I was destined to live *different* from the life I am living?" Then, focus on how the energies of our lives were magnetized to attract our present experience and ask, "How are the energies of the people, places, and things in my life either aligned or misaligned with my True Destiny? How do I raise my frequency to maintain the healthy balance of the ego's changeful outer realities, and the unchanging inner reality of my True Self."

An Endless Sea of Broken Hearts

Our hearts are officially broken … if we declare it so. It is not enough to merely survive a death blow. We must redefine our life purpose and re-examine our relevance. We can't live holding on to who we once defined ourselves to be. We can't go back to a world that no longer exists. We cannot return to what does not exist anymore. When the world changes, we must change too, otherwise we will not survive. If we cannot adjust, Natural Selection will assist in the process and provide a reset.

With so much trending talk of the vilified ego, we must examine our true relationship with our ego self to determine whether or not hunting and killing it is for our highest good. "Ego" is not limited to the narrow definition of a conceited, arrogant, self-absorbed type, who looks down upon others. Everybody has one. The ego is our personal sense of self, the idea we have about who we are. They exist in all shapes and sizes, brands and labels, and most are generic, cookie-cutter types that become the scenery but never the scene.

Identity consciousness starts with, "I am" … "I am this, or that, or not." It operates through the *mind*sets of countless identities that become the masks we wear, become attached to, and believe ourselves to be. Then we firmly affix the barcode to cover our Third-Eye and become a marketable product that we brand, label, and market to the world through the bars of the prison cell we built and locked ourselves inside of. The bars are made of race, ethnicity, gender, religion, job, career, belief systems … not real to the Essential Self. These masks of identity require our belief in them for their survival. When our disbelief in them begins to dissolve them, where do they go?

The ego self travels on a self-imposed timeline, consumed by the fear of destabilization and annihilation, always fearing the day the mask slips. It is needy, emotional, attention, and approval seeking. It craves acceptance, validation, and approval. It is willing to compromise moral integrity to conform, to "win." It craves importance and recognition without possessing anything of substance to deserve it.

On the other hand, a healthy ego gives us self-esteem that keeps our standards high as a human being. We honor the body temple as the container. The question is which self. The vehicle self, or the driver of the vehicle True Self with a capital "S?"

In cases of mass ego death, *something* or *someone* has landed a death blow with the intention of erasing our existence, crushing it, and changing the subject of our personal and collective being. Now the entire world is reeling, looking with a sense of wonder at our own self redefinition in a world that suddenly got redefined by a cartoonish standard. We don't have to hunt it and kill it. Time is killing it. Still, in the clutches of this mass physical death and mass ego death, how do we reclaim viable existence, redetermine our value, and restore our self-esteem to the levels we need to affect a healing.

The ego marks the intersection where the two seas meet … at the crossroads of Light and matter. We have already determined that it is not to be feared or necessarily destroyed. We maintain that the realization of the nature of the True Self gives us the tools required to train it like an unruly toddler. It must be made to understand that it is not the boss of us. Once that is established, we will show it how beautifully complementary it can be as a vehicle of manifestation of the True Self. The ego can then radiate the full spectrum of their combined Light, rather than busy itself seeking to eclipse it.

Everything has two sides, including ourselves. On one side is Love and Union with The Divinity … and on the other side, there are the whispered secrets of contracts and hate laced deals with the antithesis of Divinity. There are shadow energies and entities, even non-physical beings and energetic viruses that will attach and ultimately consume the person who is open enough to host them. They are known by various names from one culture to another, throughout the world.

Common energetic influences:

- *Wetiko* is a term with roots in the culture of First Nation Indigenous tribes. It refers to a highly contagious virus that invades a human's mind and can make them completely lose control. It is a virus of selfishness, an energy that is an enemy of humanity, manifesting as the absence of conscience, empathy, and compassion. They suffer from a form of malignant egofrenia, demonstrated by the embrace of hateful, elitist, racist, sexist, xenophobic, and homophobic philosophies or belief systems. They insatiably feed on the low vibrational, negative qualities of humans. Its existence is dependent upon the blindness of its host;

- *Daemon* is a Jungian term that refers to the demon of our shadow. This covetous, power-hungry energy, obsessed with domination and control over others, feeds off of hatred, jealousy, greed, envy, violence, and lack of empathy. It takes pleasure from the pain and suffering of others;

- *Djinn* refers to a class of shapeshifting, malefic spirits of the lower realms made of fire and air, who are able to possess, seduce, or influence humans to behave in ways contrary to humanity;

- *Rakshasa* is a Sanskrit term translated in English that means "injurer." They are shapeshifting, possessing, vampiric, demonic spirits that feed on human energy, flesh, and spirit.

What these forces use to operate:

- an invitation;
- portals to gain entry into our energy field;
- a resonant frequency, energy, and vibration to attach to;
- an energetically compatible environment filled with intense emotions;
- locations, substances, occasions, known or unknown mediums, celestial and karmic events;
- triggers to enable them to spark the release of extreme emotions to feed on;
- the blindness of the host to the fact that they are under a spell.

How do we protect ourselves?

- study the nature of their "spell work" and how their subliminal influences operate in and take over our lives if we are not vigilant in maintaining spiritual wellbeing. Self witness how the manifestations of their energy operate within us. Their very existence depends on the blindness of the host to the fact that they are under a spell;
- read, FEARLESS; PSYCHIC SELF DEFENSE: Transcend the Fear of Spiritual Warfare, *available @ amazon.com and dreamuniversalmedia.com;*
- enhance our natural intuitive process to activate GPS-styled guidance away from such pockets/vortices of energy;
- avoiding their hosts and their environments;
- know that they hate cleanliness, goodness, love, union, compassion, and freedom. Cultivate the highest standards of humanity. Become everything they hate. They hate our humanity … the True Beauty of Light embodied;
- increase our knowledge of how triggers and provocations operate. That way we can develop coping mechanisms that will help us skillfully neutralize these micro-attacks by minimizing our availability to feeling compelled to react in a certain manner;

- they can only manipulate and trigger that which is already within us. We all have that latent virus within. With the True Self as the "observer" we can sense, identify, and civilize our reactions to triggers;

- maintain the hovering, *objective observer* perspective, not to judge or condemn, but to ask, "Why did I think, do, say, feel, become … that? Who am I, as I am thinking, doing, saying, feeling, becoming … that?" Channel the question and the energy through the cleansing filter of the Heart Essence and accept the healing it offers;

- identify and dismiss thought-forms and "thought-form clouds" that manifest on a full spectrum of behavior that ranges from "inappropriate" to "savagely inhumane";

- they can energetically influence, magnify, applaud, and reward our transgressions, while they are keeping a running account of the karmic debt that they will probably end up helping collect from us.

They are the conduits of the Dark Night of the Soul, the womb of our rebirth, and the Temple of our enlightenment. Time is not on their side, and the Light awaits them, visiting like a thief in the night.

Characteristics of influence and interference:

- Selfish;
- Deep-seated arrogance;
- Entitlement;
- Privilege;
- An insatiable hunger that feeds on hate, shame, fear, and anger;
- Lack of empathy;
- Easily offended;
- Unforgiving;
- Cruel;

- Sullen;
- Ill-tempered;
- Predatory;
- Superficial;
- Extremely materialistic values;
- No moral compass;
- Self-conscious of image;
- Harshly judgmental of self and others;
- Gossips;
- Status conscious;
- Compromises character for approval of others;
- Paranoid about the judgment of others;
- Fake;
- Shallow and one-dimensional;
- Violent;
- Prone to narcissism;
- Prone to racism;
- Prone to sexism;
- Prone to ableism;
- Prone to embrace Xenophobic philosophies;
- Prone to embrace Homophobic philosophies;
- Provocateurs;
- No conscience;
- Sadistic;
- Abusers of power;
- Withholding;
- Critical;
- Untruthful;
- Manipulative and controlling;

- Gaslighting;
- Accusing, blaming others, and never wrong or taking responsibility for actions;
- Insecure, engages in unfavorable comparisons of self and others;
- Inferiority complex;
- Power hungry;
- Takes pleasure in exalting themselves over others;
- Jealous;
- Fiercely competitive;
- Controlling;
- Disparaging of self and others; they demean the purest of efforts;
- They inspire feelings of worthlessness in others;
- They will make you hyper-aware of your every shortcoming;
- Belittle your successes and accomplishments and magnify your failures;
- Energy vampires;
- Targeting others with their projections;
- Bullying as a means of control and torture;
- Saboteur of dreams;
- Lack of basic social skills or propriety;
- Small talkers to avoid intimate or revealing conversation or connection;
- Experts at social and personal distancing, leaving their victims empty and drained of vital life-force;
- They love to see you fail and enjoy orchestrating your downfall;
- Impeccable timing (targeting times of both crisis and joy);
- Treacherous;
- A specific blindness to possessing any of these characteristics;
- Selfish.

Note that I started this list with "selfish," and I ended it with "selfish." If you take that word and work your way down the list, you will find that every bullet point involves a type of self-centeredness that harms the self and others. A person under the influence of or possessed by Wetiko tends to seek positions and situations that give them power and authority over others. The illusion they cast will ultimately destabilize and reveal how difficult, even dangerous, they are to be around.

People infected with this deadly, non-local virus of the mind and spirit, tend to be desecrators of sacred trusts. Under this powerful spell, they can devise Judas-styled betrayals charged with the energy of your soul's crucifixion. Unlike Judas, they will feel no remorse, they relish in your destruction, and emotionally abandon you like no one would a dog they decided had stopped "fetching" properly. They can be anyone … friends, family, co-workers, and relationship partners. If you have one in your life, soon, the biggest bully in your life will be in your mirror. By the time you uncover their intricate web of lies and manipulations, they will have robbed you of every trace of your self-esteem, colonized everything good in your life, and cast you to the outside looking in, believing it was somehow all your fault. They will take pleasure in your demise, claim victory for your annoying display of brokenness, and leave you to drift away into the sea of the forgotten ones. A Wetiko influenced or possessed individual's natural habitat is the lower realms of the Dark Night of the Soul experience.

Their goals:

- To keep you blinded to the fact that you are under their spell ;
- They want you to sabotage your own life;
- They want you to poison everything you cherish;
- They want you to alienate those who care about you;
- They want you to distrust your own mind and sound judgment;
- They want you to hate yourself;
- They want you to unfavorably compare yourself to others;

215

- They don't want you to exist;
- They want you to forget who you are;
- They want you to forget who you are;
- They want you to forget who you are.

The Wetiko influenced or possessed can, and will, push the strongest person to their shattering and ultimate ego death. The antidote for this evil is the exorcism of the energy that caused it; however, an ounce of prevention is worth a pound of cure. The Self-Inquiry practice of meditation and contemplation is one of the most direct routes that I can think of to administer a powerful healing to the Heart Chakra, the Seat of Divinity. If we can manage to self-regulate using a mystical healing discipline, we can avoid drowning in their chaos. Instead, we will rise in Love with who we really are, able to enter into Realms of Consciousness that they have no access to because of their low vibrational frequency.

It is not ego, but healthy Self-esteem that is required to cultivate a grounded, self-nurturing, and loving relationship with the reflection in our psychological mirrors. We can resist this viral, airborne disease, the likes of which have caused the fall of entire civilizations. We all possess a shadow side, hidden in the blind spots of our subconscious mind, but we are the ones who determine whether or not we choose to give it power over our lives. Our responsibility is to be the ever-mindful witness and observer of it. The observer is the True Self. If we don't, we risk falling into a collective psychosis that leaves us all lost in plain sight. Nothing is stronger than the Light of the human spirit because we have the ability to connect with divinity directly.

How to purge and heal from Wetiko influences:

- Resist the blindness that sustains their existence through self-witnessing and Self -Inquiry meditation. Once you see the blindness, the cleansing has begun.

You have taken away what they feed upon, and they lose interest;

- Become fully accountable for your own poisoned energy;
- Resist mislabeling this malignancy using benign words such as darkness, mischief, horrible, and scary. Call it what it is. It is *evil*. Label it correctly, and it is easier to dispel. Make sure you do not use it as a projection or judgment against others. Resist being blind to the fact that it is in our mirrors and in our nature. Acknowledge its purpose in our lives and observe in ourselves how it triggers us. Choose Light. Choose Love;
- Cultivate a stronger relationship with Divinity;
- Set your intention. Your intention is to starve it;
- Commit to a spiritual/mystical healing practice;
- Perform a healing ritual, according to your own mystical or spiritual tradition;
- Understand that it is not an event. It is a process;
- Release vain expectations;
- Do not fall into the frequency of anger or hate, even though you may feel it is justified;
- Embrace humility. Release any need for validation, praise, and attention. Give others the chance to discover your Light;
- Practice radical Gratitude;
- Practice radical Compassion;
- Release attachment;
- Release aversion;
- Release fear and rage;
- Release the voice of the ego's mind chatter;
- Release blame;
- Release revenge;
- Release the attachment to winning;
- Release the fear of losing;
- Release shame;

- Silence the voice of the inner critic;
- Stay in the Now;
- Remain as the True Self.

Stone Meditation

The Heart Chakra
The Rose Quartz Crystal
The Cleansing

The Rose Quartz crystal is commonly used in energy healing treatments to restore wellbeing in cases of emotional trauma. On the other side of a Dark Night of the Soul experience, its alchemical properties are known to assist in dissolving energetic obstructions in the subtle body. These blockages are due to residual negative energy left behind by the experience of fear, pain, anger, and resentment. Its energies correspond with those of the planet Venus and the Fourth/Heart Chakra. Treatments using this powerful crystal can have a healing effect on the function of the heart, lungs, circulatory system, fertility, sexual dysfunction, depression, and migraines. It can also help balance Yin/Yang energies and cleanse, align, and heal each chakra to restore their correct vibratory frequency.

- Associated Crystals – Amethyst, moonstone, and jade;
- Candle Color – Pink or Green;
- Element – Earth and Water;
- Flowers and Plants – Rose, daisy, and lilac;
- Herbs, Incenses, and Oils – Rose, echinacea, mugwort, and ylang-ylang.

The Rose Quartz crystal is imbued with properties associated with:

- Intensification of positive Fourth/Heart Chakra energies;
- Healing from emotional injury in personal relationships;
- Radiating the energies of Unconditional Love;
- Offering a higher definition of Love from a Universal perspective;
- Inspiring sovereign inner peace, confidence, courage, faith, and hope;
- Promoting Self-esteem, Self-acceptance, and Self-Love;
- Alleviating the emotional pain of loneliness, rejection, and betrayal;

- Lowering stress levels resulting from emotional suffering;
- Assisting in healing from narcissistic abuse;
- Healing from overwhelming feelings of fear, guilt, and resentment;
- Restoring balance after intense experiences of anger, spite, jealousy, and envy;
- Freedom from the grip of addictions, obsessions, and compulsions;
- Encouraging forgiveness, kindness, tolerance, empathy, and compassion;
- Healing of the inner child from childhood trauma, neglect, and emotional abuse;
- Assisting with dream recall and heart-centered meditation.

These stones are alive and engage in the exchange and communication of energy. Respect, protect, and preserve their integrity by caring for them properly. Among techniques used in protocol for caring for Rose Quartz crystals:

- Cleanse and refine the life-force of crystals used in healing therapy and meditations. Deep cleansing can occur by means of prayerfully exposing them to the light of the Sun, the Moon, and/or the smoke of herbs/sage/sweetgrass/rose incense/palo santo, and soaking them in salt water;
- The practitioner may choose to use tones and frequencies (sound activations) best suited for specific types of healing and for clearing any negative energies that may have been absorbed by the crystal;
- A Rose Quartz crystal contains chambers through which the energy and breath of prayers, meditations, and affirmations may pass;
- A Rose Quartz crystal emits a healing Light that can be emitted when a connection is made with our own inner Light.

In the wake of unimaginable oppression by forces beyond human perception, mass ego death is leaving individuals as well as the collective feeling unsafe, insecure, helpless, and alone. After a lifetime of overt and subliminal assault against our authenticity in this human form, we have all had the proverbial rug snatched from under our feet. It matters not even a little bit the theories about who, what, when, where, and why … We are challenged to go into survival mode and salvage even a shred of identity as our former self. That is not 100% a bad thing. If who we believed ourselves to be was limited only to a reflection in the mirror, we were nothing but an animated cadaver anyway. So that shell got checked at the door like a coat at a winter party. Winter is here. The party is over. And it is cold outside. We are still wearing our coat. It is our coat, and in an unattached way, we are becoming aware that it is our garment … It is not our True Self. The question is, how do we make this work? How do we restructure our lives from the scattered pieces as we straddle the threshold between life and death, in this unholy war battling deadly viruses of the mind, body, and spirit?

It is bad enough that the lives of the world are intermittently placed on pause, and all realities are shifting like sand underfoot, threatening our physical survival. At the same time, we find ourselves trapped on the set of a " Mean Girls" movie, feeling as though we are sitting alone at the table in the high school cafeteria. Even the ones who do get "chosen" and accepted have gone through enough in life to now know how that cafeteria table felt.

A world classless culture of bullies has undermined the most basic levels of self-esteem and had every description of "human" feeling inadequate as a being, unfit, unaccepted, unworthy of being on this planet. The carnival barkers and bullies sling vitriol from behind their masks and costumes … with an agenda so profane we have no choice but to either evolve or dissolve. Let's define a "bully." A bully may use verbal, physical, or cyber assaults with the intention to coerce, threaten, abuse, dominate, or intimidate. This can happen within families, among friends, in communities, in institutions of education, and in the workplace. They choose their "victims" based on an imbalance of power or perceived differences … primarily having to do with mind/body identification … some physical, mental, or emotional vulnerability. Then from a false social construct, used as a platform of influence, a target is selected and literally tortured with no other goal but to witness the suffering and lend a sense of superiority to the torturer. The targets of these cruel and cowardly attacks are often left emotionally embattled and struggling to restore damaged self-esteem. In efforts to re-establish shattered self-esteem, one must:

- Acknowledge the breakage;
- Be patient and know that healing takes as long as it takes;
- Make recovery a priority;
- Take back control over your life;
- Seek professional support;
- Seek the help of trusted spiritual counsel;
- Do not self-isolate;
- Seek fellowship with supportive family and friends;
- Seek the revelation of your life purpose;
- Embrace change to align your life with your True Destiny, not to impress others;
- Motivate yourself toward new paths of personal growth;
- Celebrate the accomplishments of your life, without attachment or aversion;
- Commit to achieving future goals, without attachment or aversion;
- Do not self-define as the projections made by insecure people with inferiority complexes;
- Determine the guidance and lesson;
- Transcend the ego self;
- Identify as Light.

As Bruce Lee said, "Be Water, my friend, Be Water" ... I say, Be LIGHT, my friend, Be LIGHT. In the Spirit of Namaste, I Meditate ... I am Light and I accept and love my True Self as Light. Ask your True Self:

- How does anyone manage to bully Light?

- Does Light generally have issues with low self-esteem?
- Can Light defend itself?
- Does Light get its feelings hurt?
- Do the mockers of Light fare well in an archetypal context?
- Does Light get depressed?
- Does Light seek to extinguish itself because someone doesn't like it?
- Can Light be victimized?
- Does Light really care about the judgments, opinions, or differences of anyone?
- Can Light be contained, controlled, trained, owned, created, or destroyed?
- Does Light require tolerance, acceptance, approval, even love?
- Does anyone stop or start Light because there is an on/off switch on a wall?

We must step into the holographic structures of our vivid imaginations and inner being and affirm … I am Light. I accept and love my True Self as Light. I see my Self and others as Light and treat my Self and others as though that is ALL I see … Light. There are no "others" … One is One.

This journey, STONE MEDITATION, is an offering to connect with that Light. It communicates that the Light we must connect with is the Light within us already, longing to be connected to the Transcendent Light of our Origin.

Follow the meditation protocol in this text and play the audio version of the Stone Meditation Transcript provided for you on YouTube by Dream Universal Media, or on the *website dreamuniversalmedia.com*

Stone Meditation Transcript

Healing of the Heart Chakra

A beautiful stone is born

of a sacred relationship

between the elements and the magic of Mother Earth

She fashioned it

in the image and likeness of her energy

combined with that of our own hearts

I am placing this beautiful

Rose Quartz Crystal

in the palm of your left hand

I close your fingers gently around it

Absorb its strength … its compassion … its vision … its love … its beauty

What if I told you it belongs to you?

It has always belonged to you

Don't you remember it?

It is pink, smooth, and cool to the touch

vibrating and pulsating at a speed that can make all of your masks disappear

along with the petty world of carnal minds

and so much needless pain and suffering

I offer you this stone

Accept it

Pull its powerful healing energy into the rhythms of your heartbeat

Inhale the energy of unconditional Love

Exhale the fear of experiencing it

Inhale the deepest feeling of "belonging"

Exhale the fear of rejection

I AM

a hungry, fiery, carnal energy, coiled and resting at the sacrum

anticipating a "wake up call" to rise

from the lower abdominal energy centers,

known as the **First and Second Chakras**,

gathering strength from the Lower Tan Dien,

the reservoir that holds vital life-force

compelled by Prana, the Breath

that pushes its way up the Seven link chain

of energy centers that sustain our existence

You are longing for Oneness with the Source of all creation

and willing to initiate this sacred vertical Journey

Consciousness rides luminous waves of crimson energy

rising from the **1st Root Chakra**

holding the keys to Life and Death

the first and final gasps of Breath

I FEEL

vibrant orange Light energy filling the **2nd Sacral Chakra**

Willful in its ways, it is the seat of our strongest passions and desires,

spinning on every brand label of false identity and fake ego

The tossing about of incessant, insatiable demands only reveals

an unbearable yearning for more than the mundane

You are more than the mind/body emotional drama of this self-made pseudo-reality,

seeking to balance the insane and profane with the worship of all that is not real,

with a secret longing for the Sacred, the Eternal, the Timeless.

I DO

invite the Soul to the **Solar Plexus, 3rd Chakra**

for Wisdom and Power,

challenged by the deceptive provocateur known as the false ego

that has the willfulness of a professional saboteur

I learn to greet success and failure with the same smile

and call them both a liar

as I commit to aim a whole lot higher

I learn to move beyond polarities

witness a delicate balance being kept

Before I point a finger at the shadows of another

I am the witness of how shadows move within myself

enough to clear a path to my Heart across the Bridge between Dreams

I LOVE

as the Light in the seat of the Eternal One,

bringing Knowledge, Remembrance, Forgetfulness,

Forgiveness, and Hope

I am the **4th Heart Chakra,**

the bridge between the upper and lower Chakras

that can either connect or sever the flow

to the Upper Chakras

The rhythm of a heartbeat

is the rhythm of creation

The scent of a rose

is the scent of the Creator,

a manifestation of mutual love

The frequency and vibration

of the Rose Quartz Crystal

is medicine for healing a shattered heart

I SPEAK

through the **5th Throat Chakra**,

communicating Truth and Reality

with the vibration of

That familiar Voice

That Knows and pronounces

all names correctly

Whether written in silence, riding on screens,

dancing to melodic songs,

manifesting through the chanting of mantras,

or whispered in sincere prayer

This Voice does not belong to matter

It precedes creation

Arising from the origin of all things known

As I surrender it to the Unknown

I am the instrument that speaks realities into being

A catalytic current moves through me

as the remote that controls

the power, the channel, the volume, the on/off and mute switch,

and all of the imagery that is displayed

on this screen called life

I Am the audio before anything ever became visual

I SEE

into all dimensions

across Time and Space

into the Prophetic Realm of Revelation

of a new Self ... of the True Self

with the vision of the **6th Chakra**

Third-Eye wide open
embracing the Oneness of all

I am the gateway to the portal through which we journey into dreamtime,
through meditation, through prayer, on the wings of astral travel
into formless existence and ethereal planes of consciousness,
From the Subtle Realms of thought-forms manifest
The invisible hand of a mystic with an artistic imagination
paints a collage of 3000 possibilities on the holographic canvas of time
Images of butterflies that thought they were caterpillars
as they spread their beautiful wings and flew away

Leave this desert mirage with its illusion and fake identities
These ungraspable, unattainable, unreal phantoms of a "self" are only real when
they are marketable, bartered, traded, counterfeit versions
of the Light-filled innocent being
that passed into this realm for a taste of this life
From the Realm of Light touching Ultimate Light
Manifesting a new vision of the vehicle through which
the True Self expresses its radiant being …
Imagine a new dream, imagine a new you

I UNDERSTAND
many secrets of the Seventh Realm
and the biggest secret I keep from myself
is that I know nothing
because it is the Realm of the Unknowable
The **7th Crown Chakra** is the veil between worlds
and the still point of my journey
to the realization of my Oneness with the Divine

in the Unknowable Realm of Akasha
where I am Unknowable too
I am unknowable as my former self
at the intersection where the Universe and soul meet

I see my luminous aura, the subtlety of my form,
in the selfless experience of union
In the ascent of my perceived self-merging with all there is
in a loving embrace

*****

Hold this beautiful Rose Quartz Crystal
in your left hand
Receive its cosmic energies
radiating compassion, love, and healing
A warm, gentle rush of pink Light moves throughout your body
infusing your entire being
with a higher love than we ever believed we could feel

What if I told you this crystal
has the power to heal the pain
of flesh and spirit
of mind and heart?

What if, with this stone,
you found yourself immersed
in the healing waters of
a vast sea of hope
a lake of dreams coming true
rivers of effervescent confidence flowing
over this new manifestation of yourself

This Stone is the key to all things beautiful
Whoever tried to make you feel you were not good enough
did not know that one day
you would have this stone

You will never again be lonely or afraid
Faith and Trust will be healed and restored
You have no need to feel inferior or superior to anyone
You suddenly find peaceful refuge in your new sense of self
as whole … complete … happy … successful …
YOUR TRUE SELF

Feel this energy
Let it course through the veins of your consciousness
whispering affirmations
Compare yourself to no one!
You are as unique as your fingerprints!
Compete with no one!
Your life is no longer a competition!
You have already won!
Now you find out that YOU
as this higher aspect of your own Self
have always been the prize
and all of the games are over!

You had disappeared into stolen, antique mirrors
exiled from all sense of home and belonging …
Back against the walls of every corner every bully had pushed you into
trying not to become who hurt you
lost in a world of troubled forms and faces
projecting their images on the screen of your Facelessness

Your ONLY mirror is the Eyes of That Which created you
Accept judgment from NO ONE!
Attach yourself to NO ONE!
Seek validation from NO ONE but THE ONE
THE BELOVED!

Your beauty is etched in Light
I know this is true
because I see you …
from the Grace of fulfilled Dharma
to the race for the cleansing of Karma
Yet, you feel like you're not good enough

What if I told you this precious stone would change your life …
Wouldn't you want it?
If I told you it would make you confident and fearless …
Wouldn't you feel like you needed it?
What if I told you it could make you
happy and beautiful,
powerful, wealthy, admired, and loved?
What if I told you that with it,
you could do anything you want in life,
be anyone you want in life,
you could not fail
you could not lose?
Wouldn't you feel like you had to have this stone?
Would you feel compelled to own it?

If I were to tell you that I have a stone, a powerful stone,
a beautiful stone, a magical stone
programmed to infuse you with a rare and positive energy …

you know you would want it!

What if I told you it would heal your heart in the broken places

and wipe the tears from your suffering face?

Would you feel like you needed it?

What if I told you

it could make you embrace and love yourself

for who you really are …

Wouldn't you want it to be yours?

*****

I hold in my left hand this Rose Quartz Crystal

I receive the healing energy of unconditional love and acceptance

I see myself engulfed in soft Emerald green Light

It surrounds my physical body

It pulses to the rhythm of the Universal heartbeat

My heartbeat rides the wave of that rhythm

to the shores of the subconscious Unseen Realms

Waves of energy gently kiss a familiar shore of awareness

The water is warm

My spirit is buoyant

My heart is no stranger to suffering

yet I have chosen to own that suffering as sacred,

as a part of the natural evolution of my soul

My heart is no stranger to joy

yet I choose to release my attachment to clinging,

and craving, and being defined by it,

made an emotional hostage of it

The tears and the smiles are two wings of the same bird

This Truth is as Sacred as the Unconditional Love of the Creator

who rejoices in the freedom of my spirit

with Compassion, Mercy, Forgiveness, and Grace

The eyes of my soul seek only the Face of the Beloved, the Most High

I release the illusion of separateness

I open my heart to receive a Higher Love

I feel the vibration and energy

of the stone I grip firmly in my hand

This healing energy

travels up my left arm

then cascades over my brokenness

into the inhale of a deep cleansing breath

In through the nose

out through the mouth

a deep cleansing breath

I hold it there … right there

I am engulfed, bathed in soothing pink Light

I accept this Light moving throughout my entire body

from the top of my head to the bottom of my feet …

back up my legs into my lower abdomen …

whirling with the beauty and grace of a Dervish mid-spin

I am filled with Light

a Light that permeates my entire being

with warm, radiant, healing energy

on every level of my existence

I am grounded and one with the Mother Earth

I am humbled by Father Time

I surrender my attachment to all but Love

I am connected to Divine Essence, the Source of all things

I observe my breath as I close my eyes and enter the Dreamtime world

My Third-Eye vision witnesses

images and stories projected

on a huge silver screen

that covers the portal

opening to the dimension,

the embrace, of the Unknowable

It is Love we all want

It is fear and ignorance that blocks it from our lives

*****

Put the stone in your right hand and prepare to let it go

Let it go!

Let go of this clinging!

With the innocence of a child

release shame and guilt

Drop the veils that hide your true beauty

Drop the defenses that isolate you

Wake up and live your life

because it matters

YOU ARE the crystal

YOU ARE the sacred space

Take a deep cleansing breath

Feel foolish for surrendering your power to a rock!

Own your happiness

Happiness is your nature.

Ramana said, "It is not wrong to seek it.

What is wrong is seeking it outside when it is inside."

A stone is of the realm of created things

no different from yourself

Be the co-Creator of your Sacred journey to Ultimate Light

Travel up and down the corridors of your sadness

Kiss that sadness goodbye and realize that somehow,

you created that too

Stand in the wisdom and beauty of your True Self

Affirm:

I don't have to return to any of my former selves

from the very first moment of my innocence

in this play of existence

Acknowledge the Voice of the Great Spirit

Free The Voice of the Unknowable Force within

without compromise

Let the rock go!

Put it down!

You don't need it anymore!

Everything you were told is in that stone,

that magic is in YOU!

Your frequency creates your Reality

*****

The Dark Night of my Soul

The self-illuminating triple darkness

that I feared, turned out to be the womb of my rebirth

What came for me left empty handed …

I feel foolish for having surrendered my power to a rock

I place my right hand over my heart

I hold sacred there all that I truly am

I feel the dreams that are dreaming of me right now

I feel the Love of the Divine seated

right here in my heart

and I affirm my Oneness with Transcendent Light

I hear the silent messages land there

I hold them

as the manifestation

of all of my hidden potential

I am the stone

I am the head cornerstone that the builders refused

Its energy dwells within me now

The power of manifestation lies within

I go within

I go within

I go within

and there

I find

my True Self

The endurance of darkness is preparation for great Light.

St. John of the Cross

Epilogue

The Longing

At some point in our lives, we humans have an innate longing for completion, and this completion cannot be experienced through the fulfillment of mundane fantasies and worldly pleasures. Instead, we must go within, to the immeasurable depths of our souls, where the Most High rests upon the throne of our heart's understanding of the existential dilemma that seeks to lift the veil and enter the portal of Knowing.

In the dark night of our longing for "home," a transformation is experienced as a painful and confusing transitional rite of passage. The unconscious reaches for the mysterious Light of a higher consciousness, and the relentless pursuit of sensory pleasures becomes void of gratification. The hunger may increase, but not the satisfaction. Finally, we find incomprehensible emptiness that seems impossible to fill. Our common senses cannot perceive what this conspiracy of subtleties is.

Immersed in deep contemplation we:

- Examine the nature of what is happening to us;
- Explore feelings that something just isn't right;
- We feel that life is not what it seems;
- Our senses cannot perceive what is suddenly and progressively wrong;
- Deep contemplation may appear to turn to chronic depression;
- Our minds try to grasp that which cannot be understood by the human intellect;
- Spiritual phenomena can occur regardless of religion or prior belief systems;
- Disinterest in excessive indulgence in unconscious, low vibrational behaviors;
- Our heart is not in what once was pleasurable;
- Deep feelings of not belonging;
- Feelings of being a misfit in what was previously familiar;

- Unable to adjust our values when clear vision reveals that strings are attached;
- Loss of appetite for the former trappings of identity.

This is not an event. It is a process of shedding off ego in layers, beginning with giving up the obsession with controlling what is not ours to control. We begin to lose our attachment to being defensive about losing who and what we thought we were, without having to have a plan for what we will be.

There may be increased interest in metaphysical practices such as:

- Meditation;
- Prayer;
- Diverse healing traditions and therapies;
- Studying religious, mystical, and spiritual sciences.

Union with the Beloved, which is the Divine, is only complete with the knowledge that the Divine is in everything and everyone. Every endeavor moves toward union between the soul and the Source of its origin. An increased awareness of it is followed by an increased acceptance of it. What the soul wants more than anything is Love. Not just any love, but a Love that is Eternal. When we become One, the emptiness is gone. The dawn will illuminate our path.

The Dark Night of the Soul experience is an initiatory rite of passage into higher planes of mystical wisdom, knowledge, and understanding. It is the crossroad where *believing* turns into *knowing*. It is not uncommon for a major shift in consciousness and belief system to arise after transcending the ego-stripping Dark Night. Mystical experiences will occur to offer evidence, guidance, and protection in all aspects of life.

From a Western perspective of obsession with the *personal*, a state of consciousness known as Turiya can be an abstract, obscure concept. Clinging to "*personal*" body-mind identification, one can still "fall" into Turiya, without there being a committed meditation practice in place. After having transcended to, or "landed" there, there is no such thing as returning to the former states of consciousness, as though it never happened. *Personality*, and the trappings that support it fall away. Once it has touched you, the longing never goes away.

Sometimes the experience of the State of Turiya is not intentional. It can occur as spontaneously as a dream, as it did in my case. It may be a rite of passage, an initiatory event that will push a reluctant soul to a stronger commitment to spiritual studies. We will all more than likely go through something in life and discover we have no one to call except That which created us from dust. A trigger event, or series of events, can cause the rug to be snatched out from under our feet. The "What happened?" trauma of a lifetime strikes like a bolt of lightning. There's nothing, and nobody left to cling to, or call … No one left to even identify as. We ask of the darkness, "Who am I?" Profound silence has no echo. No longer identified with the body, the past, the future, or even the story of the "self" of our prior understanding. What do we do then?

I don't recommend waiting for a spontaneous enlightenment experience to achieve Self-Realization. It is wiser to personalize a spiritual practice or sadhana that represents a willing submission to the Will of the Highest Power and Force of Divinity. Lower states of consciousness will wave a white flag of surrender. It happens when we have given up our willful fight in the name of our personhood, usually following the perception of being conquered in a long-fought battle. In such an advanced state of surrender, forces are already in place as a protective circle of interminable energy, waiting for the ego to dissolve, and for an unspoken petition for help.

The willfulness of the "fighter" has been cast into the subtle realms of non-personal existence, and the shield in the quest for autonomy that had been raised, even to the Face of the Absolute, is lowered. A gentle sweeping away by a circular current of warm, shimmering, effervescent energy whirls a weary spirit, like a Dervish, up into the arms of the Beloved ... the Creator. Remembrance of Oneness with The Absolute eclipses any thoughts of separation. A gentle vibration ensues, a cleansing breath becomes identity into the stillness beyond form, piercing the veil of Maya's illusions.

It could occur as an absorption or dissolution into the Ultimate Oneness. It may be what is considered a complete obliteration of the identity as the former self ... to be slain in the spirit ... to die before dying. It is an annihilation, an extinction of the 'self,' commonly called Fanaa, or more extremely Fanaa al Fanaa, in Arabic/Persian/Hindi/Urdu, which basically means the ego's destruction of all destructions. Turiya is the net below the fall ... you just know that somewhere there is an exotic name for the feeling, even if you have never even heard the word "Turiya" uttered.

Yogic practices have long touted the miraculous states of consciousness available to practitioners. It was never my aspiration to be a Yogi, though I have always admired their endurance and strength of commitment to their mystical tradition. My interest in meditation began early in life in my Martial Arts training. It improved my strength, focus, and endurance. Later in life, I found meditation to be a remedy for a sleep disorder. Years later, in the wake of a serious car accident, I experienced relief from chronic pain, using guided meditation. I studied Vipassana, and other paths of meditation with the understanding that, as the body needs breath to live, the mind needs stillness to sustain equilibrium.

Stillness and mindfulness can lead to a state beyond states, where there is more available than just maintenance. Most profound was my realization that the experience of the True Self is our natural state ... the egoless, formless, Timeless, awareness that we are. Body-mind identity falls away. We discover that to invest our faith in "flesh" is to ride a rotting corpse into the hell of hungry ghosts and watch our lives become a shadow in the Sun. Once the final link in the chain of our attachment to form and flesh is broken … the longing sets in … the longing for the consciousness of our home of Origin. What could be called plummeting into an existential crisis, can instead be experienced as rising into exalted realms of consciousness, no longer available to seductive whispers from the domain of illusion.

If we do not commit our every moment of every day to living our lives in the Ether instead of the mirror, we will be consumed by the most dehumanizing and degrading energies most of us have ever experienced. Like a virus, the idea has spread that our reflections in the mirror are of more value than our perception of who we really are. It is not a New Age concept to be defined as the True Self (Timeless, formless being) … not the one in the selfies … nor the one that feels possessed by strangers who seek to extinguish your humanity for profit. We are being rewired to be more concerned with, and defined by image than we are energy. As long as we think that what we see in the mirror conforms to the projections on our flat screens and magazines … by the most juvenile of standards ... we think we are okay. What a cage to be confined in. What a zoo to become a spectacle in. We ignore the odious, fixated, self-debasing, judgmental, competitive, toxic energies that cannot be captured in our selfies. We long to go deeper.

We don't have to accept the so-called 'new norm' of it being considered civilized to rob self and others of the most basic levels of our collective humanity. Our reality has been reduced to algorithms in programs with an agenda to rewire the circuitry of our brains, to be defined based on the judgments and conditioning of others. *Now* we are supposed to believe that how we are *perceived* is the sum total of who we really are and what our true value is. Our identities are cosmetic, vanity, and status-based projections of our "owners" now, while our humanity turns into a compost dump. We are more than the stench of this mass hypnosis, this dangerous intoxication, this spiritual possession. We are not the selfie. We are the True Self, in all of its Timeless glory. As the True Self we are "Self"less. The only useful purpose this parasitic culture can serve is to rip off the veil of Maya and expose her fraudulent deceptions. It is possible to disappear to the illusion, and awaken in the Timeless Realm of Turiya, beyond the plane of names and forms.

Turiya is always there, just behind each of the lower states of consciousness, longing to be known, patiently awaiting the ultimate encounter with the experience of liberation. We may fall to the other side of the veil of illusions again, but our essence is forever altered. The existential question, "Who am I?" is not a question to be answered. It is a question to make the inquirer disappear. In the manifestation of the True Self, there is nobody left to fall into former states of consciousness. The spirit of renunciation is not required. There is nothing and no one left to renounce anything. There is no one left to even remember what happened. All that is left behind is the one left to tell others the story of the disappearing … and the selfless longing. All that is left is the Oneness, and the Dawn, peeking out from behind the soul's Dark Night, dissolving into the embrace of The Divinity.

"Man is an infinite circle whose circumference is nowhere, but the center is located on one spot; and God is an infinite circle whose circumference is nowhere, but whose center is everywhere."

~ Swami Vivekananda ~

The longing that was all-consuming turns to BE-longing and knowing, That which created us is sufficient to sustain us, to protect us, and to heal us. What was an ever-deepening sense of homesickness for a home there was no recollection of, gradually fades into the enlightened acceptance of the knowledge that this is **NOT** our home. That is one of the offerings of Turiya, once experienced. A rising level of fear of placing trust in flesh sets in. A growing sense of estrangement from the familiar things, people, places, family, friends turns into a life that morphs like a Salvador Dali painting and eventually recedes from memory. All that is left is the pain of intense yearning, a longing for the existential point of origin, reunion with the Beloved Essence of Divinity.

Nothing exceeds the Omnipotence of The God. There are no associates, deified partners, equals, individuated attributes, or personifications worthy of bowing down to or worshiping, but The God. That is all we have. The connection with That is all we are. The extinction of the "s"elf and surrender to the "S"elf reflects the rapture of Oneness with the Divine One.

Annihilate the "s"elf of our lower understanding. Negate the small self, render it extinct, as though it had only been a confusing dream. Treat it as sheer vanity to have believed it was real in the first place. The quest for Oneness with the Divine is a primordial yearning. As we acknowledge that we are born of and into duality, we accept that the experience of, and as, both the darkness and the Light, is the price we pay for existence. To construct a life of avoiding, hating, and cursing the darkness, is to deny a foundational element of our own being. It is as self-defeating and futile as the two sides of the Yin and Yang getting into an argument. As Time and Space folds in upon itself, trapping us in its creases, we must *become* the Light we seek. The enveloping fold called The Dark Night of the Soul is a transitory experience that reveals, on the other side of the coin of existence, a third side. It is the side that wraps itself around the two sides and holds them together. Turiya is the Realm of that Limitless Self-Illuminating Light Potential, inherent within the Sacred Triple Darkness … the tree within the seed. It is the secret place of the Most High, The Realm of Divinity, breathlessly whispering into the subtlest chamber of the heart before its first beat. Where That Light comes from is the promise of Eternity. All we have to do is find it, finding us. Not only is there a mutual seeking, there is a bond of mutual realization that we are always, already ONE with That Light.

What we seek is seeking us.

~ Rumi ~

After my unsolicited experience of Turiya, I understand the concept of the "*longing* for Oneness with the Divine One." This sacred longing is the natural state of the True Self seeking a connection we will never find among the names and forms of others, not even in our own. We do not have to *go* there to *be* there. We are *already* there. All we have to do is *realize* that we are, and the veil is violently ripped off, revealing the total annihilation of all that we believed in and thought that we were. When we have transcended our darkest night and ascended into the Realm of Turiya, however we get there, we accept that Turiya is the True State of our consciousness and the foundational reality of all other states.

Our challenge is to resist identifying as what we are not and embrace the Eternal Reality of Turiya, the natural state of who we really are. Pull her into the heart of our longing and realization that, from the womb to the tomb, the Dark Night of the Soul is not an event to fear, to avoid, or escape. It is the soul's longing for The Light. The Point at which Ultimate Light intersects the Light of the True Self, *longing becomes belonging.* The longing is only a state of seeking the experience of our connection with The Divine One. The longing is sacred. The longing *is* the connection.

The Offering

I thought I had reached the end of the book. I closed the document with the greatest sense of completion!

After all:

- I had selflessly shared my brokenness and despair to prove that others were not alone and that life can deliver brokenness to some of the strongest among us;
- I documented the symptoms and manifestations of a classic "Dark Night of the Soul" experience and confirmed the wakeup call on the other side of the incredible violence of its ravages;
- I shared my amazing story of how I survived to see the dawn;
- I shared that my survival was not in any way due to my 'person'al strength or spiritual superiority ... It was an intervention;
- I had been carried away to Turiya;
- I did a lot of research to find out what Turiya even is, and shared my findings;
- I had shared parallels between my phenomenal Turiya experience and my prior meditation experiences;
- I would hopefully be successful at lighting a lantern and shining a Light into someone else's perceived darkest hour;
- I had found the way out of suffering ... and shared my new secret with the world of Dark Night travelers;
- I shared the fact that we do not have to suffer;
- This excited little voice from the West cried out of the abyss, "Just go to Turiya and feel all better!" ... like it was a spa trip self-care escape;
- I did and said all the things.

Then I got into a conversation with a very wise friend. His is the kind of conversation that one must attend with a notebook and pen, then be prepared to do

research. I shared that I had completed my book and closed the document …
FINALLY!!! I expressed the healing, the refuge, the escape that I had found in
Turiya, and how this was only the beginning of finding a different perspective from
which to view the overwhelming horrors of this Maya illusory world experience,
without just breaking. He was happy for my sense of accomplishment and then
began to propose a next level perspective that gave me another spiritual vocabulary
list and started a new research project.

The conversation started about the healing potential of electrical currents,
frequencies, and tones of mantras and prayers; how many repetitions per year to
unblock a chakra; how many to charge one's Self to vibrate at a frequency so
powerful that a person of lower vibrational frequency would have to sit on the
opposite side of a room to keep from feeling "burned." He talked about "spanda," a
term that refers to a heart tremor or vibration, a primordial vibration of the
Universe, and of our being. The conversation turned to a subject that made me
know that, not only was this book not complete without at least mentioning it …
neither was I complete, without understanding the sacredness of a higher
perspective.

The word "Paraklisis" will probably always haunt me. I had never heard it
before. It makes reference to a particular type of service in which the Holy Spirit is
called upon in a "supplication" or "petition" specifically for the well-being of the
living in times of discouragement, illness, despair, mourning, trials, and
tribulations. It is a prayer for intercession and salvation for those who are being
"crucified" by, and in this world. It is not done for self-serving reasons. It is done
for others. It is done on behalf of the collective … for everyone.

My research turned up that "Paraklisis" intercessions are sought through
ceremonial chanting, hymns, sacred songs, sounds, verses, voices, and words,
petitioning to console, comfort, give refuge, courage, and safe space, as God would,
and has given us. It is said that the most popular Paraklisis is addressed to the Holy

Spirit and that these services are identifiable throughout numerous spiritual and cultural paths and expressions, differing only in methods of traditional practice.

In Biblical scriptures, Paul describes *paraklisis* as a chain reaction, saying that God "consoles us in our affliction so that we can console those who are in any affliction with the consolation with which God has consoled us." In that context, the word is translated as intercessor or advocate in addition to comforter. The word is a compound that means *"near"* and *"to call,"* so it means literally *"to call near."* In its verb form, it can mean a variety of techniques of calling near, to not only comfort, but also to encourage, pray, invite, or implore. Someone can *parakaleo* when they are witnessing someone in deep states of pain and peril and want to reach out to them in a manner to comfort or console, and someone may *parakaleo* to God when in need of the intimate embrace of Divine. It seems to inevitably involve a claim, a sense of intimacy with the presence of the Divine One.

I was forced to reassess my spiritual goals. Yes, I was graced with and offered healing by a spontaneous experience of the transcendent state of consciousness known as Turiya. Yes, I am eternally grateful for that gift … grateful enough to commit myself to learn every aspect of the actual meditative process and practice of it, from its tradition of origin. But, NO, I will not singularly pursue a spiritual practice only for relief from my own suffering. NO, I will not use a sacred meditation practice as a method of escape to other realms for the purpose of avoiding the witnessing of the suffering in this realm. NO, I will not seek to desensitize myself to the suffering I witness, using mystical forms of meditation. I will commit to an inclusive practice that sets an intention to encompass sentient beings everywhere, such as the Metta Loving Kindness Prayer. The intention of the Metta meditation practice is to alleviate suffering on a global level and petition for World Peace.

- We must not desensitize ourselves to the suffering of others;

- We must not seek to escape the witnessing of what we have incarnated here to witness;
- We must not lack empathy and hide from our responsibility and spiritual duty to call out into the dark matter of the void for help, not just for our own survival, but for the salvation of ALL.

I am a student of Yogic philosophies, but I am not a yogi. I have too much respect for the ancient tradition to appropriate or pass myself off as an aspirant, based on an experience of Grace that was bestowed upon me. However, I don't feel that anyone has to be a Yogi to experience certain states of consciousness if it is your fate/dharma/karma to do so. If it is destiny, you may get snatched up and tossed into a state with a name and description you will have to google to identify, just like what happened to me.

The goal is Awareness, Mindfulness, and Intention … It is all good. But we cannot use sacred practices to engage in escapism from the witnessing of the suffering of others. If our practice is for the purpose of desensitizing ourselves to the pain, sorrow, and grief of others, it is incomplete. The sound current of a sacred mantra can be used to burn Karma, but should not be used to create more karma for having ignored the cries of those in despair when we could have done something to help them. The Universe has a way of delivering that package right back to our doorstep, no matter what form of door we try to hide behind. We must not hide in the emptiness, the nothingness, from what is ours to witness. The Dark Night of the Soul will always issue in a golden dawn. We are here to experience. We are here to witness. It is all a part of consciousness. We are here to learn the sacredness of surrender to the Will of the Highest Consciousness. We will all, at some point in life, be forced to suffer with circumstances we cannot change. We will all find our backs against the proverbial wall … helpless, in times of great transition. It is not personal. It is the changeful nature of life. The price we pay for existence is understanding that everything is *always* in transition.

During any Dark Night experience, remember this Triple Darkness is Self-Illuminating, and it is not just emptiness. Something is there. If darkness was all that was there, then Who said, *"Let there be Light?"* Aspire to go Beyond the Dark Night of the Soul into the Realm of Turiya, the Realm of Divinity, for Light, for Healing, for recharging the battery of consciousness. We must be still as the sky, not the clouds that pass across it. We do not have to succumb to the sorrow to observe it with the intention of healing. We abide as the True Self, in faith, in hope, in firm meditation and prayer, not just for ourselves, but for all of humanity. We must not forget who we are. We are everyone and everything.

Service as Meditation

After you have aggressively addressed the cause or causes of your state of mind and spirit, it is time to consider freeing yourself from the bondage of it. Heal yourself, then reach out to others who are struggling to survive the same thing. Extending your healing energies to others will have the effect of changing your energy field and magnetizing it to attract a better life. First, reach out to *yourself* because you cannot give of an empty or broken cup. It can be hard to accept the reality that you are suffering from fear, denial, shame, or facing hardships beyond your control that limit your options.

- Strengthen your spiritual practice;
- Seek spiritual help and healing;
- The existence of any unsafe or abusive environment must be acknowledged;
- Seek professional advice and treatment;
- Reach out for help among supportive family and friends;
- Make every effort to address the underlying issues that led to being in such a dysfunctional situation;
- Determine what is pushing you into such misery, and remove it from your life;
- Safely extricate yourself from the situation that is causing your suffering;
- Resolve it by whatever means necessary and available.

Whether it is an abusive relationship, workplace situation, or living environment, don't let anything or anyone stop you from believing in yourself. Keep your head up. You are stronger than you know. You can change your mind. You can change your life. You can change your circumstances. Don't give up.

When you are sure you have recovered sufficiently enough to be of service to others, the best way to heal personal suffering is to cultivate a consciousness that inspires you to reach out in some way to help another through their Dark Night.

There are many ways that the spirit of giving can be expressed. The beginning of healing from trauma and grief is to align yourself with service providing agencies that share your level of compassion, and find a way to volunteer. You will be amazed at the dramatic shift of energy in your life. In all of our endeavors and ambitions, if we do not in some way seek to be of service to others, we have not earned our place on the grand stage of this phase of existence. Our first act of service is to embrace the Sacred Law of Impermanence as it sparks the awakening to our Essential State of being. We must accept that everything is always changing. It is not change that makes us suffer. It is the clinging to the illusion of an unchanging reality that clouds our minds and causes our suffering.

As we suffer from our own experience of fear and loss, we must understand that becoming a healing in the lives of others is the answer to maintaining our own well-being. We cannot effectively serve The God or humanity without the study of our own Light as well as our own shadows, viewing everything through the filter of duality. One is not good and the other evil, for That Which Created all, created both.

Every day we engage in the same battle that began with our creation, the struggle to keep a healthy balance between our physical and non-physical Self. We are given help on either side of the veil, between seen and unseen existence, on this sacred journey. There are Astral and Earth-bound beings that are commissioned to serve humanity in keeping our delicate balance. Our willingness to serve humanity as an offering is our passport to a state of being that lives in love and service. To do this great work, we shift gears in our earthly vehicle, accepting that the mystical understanding of both our material and spiritual attributes represent the balancing act that causes us to exist.

There is no such thing as a coin with only one side. We can live our lives like a misspent, one-sided coin if we do not accept responsibility for bringing our natural contradictions into union. That union must then realize its union with the

Unknowable. The committed search for the Source of the Light that we are is the beginning of our service to the Creator. To humble ourselves in service to creation is the Ultimate union with the Creator. The choice to do so causes our rise into the empathic energies of a Light Worker.

A Lightworker is one who has chosen to become an instrument dedicated to the development of the expertise required to enable others to perceive and receive energies and frequencies that are just out of reach to them. The Lightworker raises his or her vibration to the level or frequency required to become the medium through which healing energies and intentions are channeled. That type of energy cannot be channeled without resulting in a healing for the medium. We must embrace the task of becoming a healing force in the world we live in.

We are living in a world that is like a dream that the Creator is having of experiencing humanity through us … as us. Through us, a family was born of the purest Love. We were even given a choice to return that love or not, secure in knowing that within the Light of our creation, there would always be that Spark of Love within us as a bond. We do not serve a God of clay. We serve an Infinite Spirit so profound Its Name can only be expressed by silence. We are not merely beings of clay but of Infinite Spirit. Clay is our temple of The Divine. Clay is also our prison. Spirit is our Ultimate Formless Reality, the Reality out of which we were born into this dream. The pain of our laborious journey on this plane of dreams and illusions is the price we must pay, in service and in sacrifice, to deserve the blessings we receive. Even the pain is sacred. The suffering is sacred. The joy is sublime.

The Self-Realized being knows no conflict between spirit and clay, knows no pain, no suffering or grief, no death. We do not succumb to the lies these illusions tell, the most terrifying of which is, "This will last forever." We expand our Light through our experience of joy and suffering in the clay prison, in which our souls abide for a time. We live in the valley of the shadow of death. Our consciousness may ascend into the realms of all Light, escaping time with a single thought. This is the process of expansion that justifies and qualifies our existence. We will ultimately return to our spiritual home with knowledge that no spirit, unborn into this carnal plane, can even comprehend.

The God allowed the manifestation of Itself to be born onto this plane of existence to experience the persecution, pain, and death that is our sacrificial offering. An archetypal crucifixion/resurrection scenario occurs every day with the rising and setting of the Sun. Because it sets and appears to disappear does not mean it does not exist anymore. These cyclical transitions are signs revealing the rising within us of the eternal Light of our awakening and our plight of service and suffering through trials and tribulations. These Yin and Yang energies keep the balance without apology. It is a testament to the magnificence of our Creator. We have a Light within that seeks to comfort, enlighten, and attend to our needs, extending out to the needs of humanity. We are One with That nurturing Light.

The prophecies of the sacred scriptures are now the headlines in the daily newspapers. I do not seek to be an alarmist. The world does not need another alarmist. I am suggesting that we strive to heal the energy in our own lives so that, in these trying times, when someone reaches out to us in a cry for help, we will have the spiritual tools and expertise to help them with an open and compassionate heart. No more is required of us than to know who we truly are. This knowledge is rewarded with the understanding that we are all the same in Essence, and that Essence is indestructible. To serve others is service to Self and The God.

The most effective form of healing from the suffering and pain of life is understanding the importance of a spiritual discipline that nourishes our soul. We are required to cultivate the ability to suspend our senses, control our passions, conquer our addiction to the immediate gratification of every fleeting desire and thought-form, and submit to becoming a less self-obsessed, self-serving person. How can we help others if we are no better off than those we are attempting to help? We take on this honor of service not just for ourselves, but for humanity in general and encourage others to do the same. We may be the next one reaching out for help and be met with the cold indifference, arrogance, or ignorance that is so common in the cultures of this world today. Indifference is beyond hatred. Arrogance is a curse. Ignorance is inexcusable.

We must observe the spiritual mandates that give us wings to transcend everything; our own pettiness, race, religion, socio-economic status, gender, sexual orientation, ethnicity, politics, skin color, and nationality. We must be the keepers of our brothers and sisters, not their judge. We must see ourselves as the magnificent creation that we are, and know that we possess the power to heal the wounds of spiritual disease.

Of course, we all have our own personal problems, more overwhelming in drama and character than ever before. If it were not for all of the confusing interference, we might all be able to raise our frequency to perceive the higher vibrations available to us to heal ourselves and others. The effect of such a shift of consciousness toward compassion and empathy would not only cause a personal healing but also manifest the healing of others through us. We are energy, surrounded by an endless sea of energy, like a wave that rises upon the ocean. It is crucial to keep our energy clean and refine our standards regarding the energies we allow ourselves to become exposed to.

There is much about the times and cultures we live in that can cause shifts in frequencies counter to our well-being, scrambling our senses, and controlling our consciousness in ways that are virtually imperceptible. The fact that it is invisible does not mean that it does not exist or is not affecting us. We may find ourselves living in reaction to things we do not think exist, just because we can't see it or prove it. If we are not paying attention, we have no idea how our limited, confused, and befuddled frequencies are creating physical and mental disease in ourselves and the people around us.

There is, and always has been, suffering in this world. Now more so than ever, it is a spiritual imperative to offer ourselves in sacrifice by committing our lives first to the service of our Creator and then to the service of creation. If our lofty goals and ambitions in life cause us to exalt ourselves over others, placing ourselves above serving others who have fallen into crisis and need, we will create for ourselves the Karma to become one of them. We will either be one of the ones administering healing, or one of the ones begging for it. Those are our choices. It is our choice as to which side of that scenario we will be on.

There are people doing The Great Work of this spiritual journey who do not even know they are doing it. There are others who can be trained to enhance the powers and skills they have hidden deep within. These latent energies only need to be triggered by some spiritual force powerful enough to cause that spark necessary to jump the gap between streams of energy, causing change. It is time that we drop the masks that divide and conquer us, threatening our very existence. If we do not remove the masks, we have no reason to fear death because that level of ignorance carries consequences that are worse than death. If we choose to live a life of such low vibration, seeking only the satisfaction of our own ego-based desires, death is redundant. We are already dead. That is the death we should fear the most.

I don't think it is advisable to use Turiya, or any other meditation practice to seek to escape the Dark Night of the Soul experience or the five stages of grief that may accompany or follow. We can experience them with impeccable courage, as we reach out for help, counseling, and guidance. The five stages of grief, *denial, anger, bargaining, depression,* and *acceptance,* take on a different meaning, and the healing is easier if they are approached in reverse. We begin with acceptance, the acceptance of who we really are and the true nature of life, as it really is. We face depression, anger, and denial in meditation and prayer, with the knowledge that nothing is more powerful than the Essential Light of the human spirit. Bargaining is dangerously willful. We chant it down. We pray it off. We affirm our connection and Oneness with Divinity. We surrender our personal will. We embrace the stages of Transcendence and Love them into Ultimate Light.

THERE IS NO END

About the Author JAI (Jāy)

With early beginnings as a published songwriter, JAI's passion has remained her poetry. She has been published in the Los Angeles Sentinel, SIC Magazine, Talisman Magazine, UCLA's NOMMO Magazine, Point of Light, The Drumming Between Us, and African Voices. Her publications by *Dream Universal Media* are listed below. *Dream Universal Media* specializes in literature, audio, and video recordings, specifically designed to heal the consciousness of mind, body, and spirit through Mystical Meditation.

JAI is a student and teacher of metaphysical sciences and many mystical healing traditions, including Tibetan, Hawaiian, Native American, African, Caribbean, Eastern, Chinese, and Japanese, all of which inspired her work. JAI continues to teach, publish, and write. Her works include;

THE TIMELESS NOW: HEALING FROM GRIEF AND LOSS
Mystical Meditation: The Sacred Law of Impermanence

FEARLESS: Psychic Self-Defense – Transcend the Fear of Spiritual Warfare

SLEEPLESS: Transcend the Fear of Sleep Paralysis

SELFLESS: TURIYA – Beyond the Dark Night of the Soul

FACELESS: THE SACRED RELATIONSHIP – How to Heal Your Relationships Through Mystical Meditation & Transpersonal Self-Counseling

LIMITLESS: MADE OF LIGHT – Your Companion Reference Book for FACELESS

SMOKE & MIRRORS: A Poetic Journey to The Higher Self

NAMELESS

SANDBOXES

DREAM UNIVERSAL JOURNAL

AUDIO AND VIDEO MEDITATIONS INCLUDE:

The Light Meditation

I Transcend my Ego Self Meditation

Stone Meditation

Turiya Meditation

JAI (Jāy), literally means "Victory" in Sanskrit, representing the Spirit of this sacred journey. Look for more at *dreamuniversalmedia.com.*

Meditation Download Instructions

To download the audio meditation included in this book go to Dreamuniversalmedia.com and select the OUR PRODUCTS page, then select the Audio Meditations section and follow the instructions.

Works Cited

Hazrat Inayat Khan. The Mysticism of Sound, Music, Power of the Word, Cosmic Language. Published by the library of Alexandria 1/1/1963

A Course in Miracles. Foundation for Inner Peace, 1985.

"Vipassana Meditation." *International Meditation Centres |Home,*
    www.internationalmeditationcentre.org/global/index.html.

Gibran, Khalil, AL-AJNIHA AL-MUTAKASSIRA, 1912
    (The Broken Wings, English Translation)

Kahlil Gibran, The Wanderer, 1932
    Alfred A Knopf, New York, New York

Gibran, Kahlil. *The Prophet.* New York: Knopf, 1952. Print.

Rumi, Jalal Al-Din, and Coleman Barks. *The Essential Rumi.* San Francisco, CA: Harper, 1995. Print.

Rumi, Jalal Al-Din, and William C. Chittick. *The Sufi Path of Love: The Spiritual Teachings of Rumi.* Albany: State U of New York, 1983. Print.

Recommended Reading

A Course in Miracles

Hazrat Inayat Rehmat Khan; The Soul's Journey

Idries Shah; The Sufis

Nisargadatta Maharaj; I Am That

Paramhansa Yogananda; Autobiography of a Yogi

(Self-RealizationFellowship)

Sri Ramana Maharshi; Who Am I?

Thich Nhat Hanh: The Pocket Thich Nhat Hanh

Sayagyi U Ba Khin; What is Vipassana Meditation

Rupert Spira: Being Aware of Being Aware

Sun Tzu and John Minford; The Art of War

C.W. Leadbeater. Man, Visible and Invisible. The Theosophical
Publishing House First Edition 1902

shhhhhhh